Other Publications:

WORLD WAR II
THE GREAT CITIES
THE WORLD'S WILD PLACES
THE TIME-LIFE LIBRARY OF BOATING
HUMAN BEHAVIOR
THE ART OF SEWING
THE OLD WEST
THE EMERGENCE OF MAN
THE AMERICAN WILDERNESS
THE TIME-LIFE ENCYCLOPEDIA OF GARDENING
LIFE LIBRARY OF PHOTOGRAPHY
THIS FABULOUS CENTURY
FOODS OF THE WORLD
TIME-LIFE LIBRARY OF AMERICA
TIME-LIFE LIBRARY OF ART
GREAT AGES OF MAN
LIFE SCIENCE LIBRARY
THE LIFE HISTORY OF THE UNITED STATES
TIME READING PROGRAM
LIFE NATURE LIBRARY
LIFE WORLD LIBRARY
FAMILY LIBRARY:
   HOW THINGS WORK IN YOUR HOME
   THE TIME-LIFE BOOK OF THE FAMILY CAR
   THE TIME-LIFE FAMILY LEGAL GUIDE
   THE TIME-LIFE BOOK OF FAMILY FINANCE

HOME REPAIR
AND IMPROVEMENT

NEW LIVING SPACES

BY THE EDITORS OF
TIME-LIFE BOOKS

TIME-LIFE BOOKS
ALEXANDRIA, VIRGINIA

Time-Life Books Inc.
is a wholly owned subsidiary of
TIME INCORPORATED

Founder: Henry R. Luce 1898-1967

Editor-in-Chief: Hedley Donovan
Chairman of the Board: Andrew Heiskell
President: James R. Shepley
Vice Chairman: Roy E. Larsen
Corporate Editor: Ralph Graves

TIME-LIFE BOOKS INC.

Managing Editor: Jerry Korn
Executive Editor: David Maness
Assistant Managing Editors: Dale M. Brown, Martin Mann
Art Director: Tom Suzuki
Chief of Research: David L. Harrison
Director of Photography: Melvin L. Scott
Planning Director: John Paul Porter
Senior Text Editors: William Frankel, Diana Hirsh
Assistant Art Director: Arnold C. Holeywell

Chairman: Joan D. Manley
President: John D. McSweeney
Executive Vice Presidents: Carl G. Jaeger (U.S. and Canada),
David J. Walsh (International)
Vice President and Secretary: Paul R. Stewart
Treasurer and General Manager: John Steven Maxwell
Business Manager: Peter G. Barnes
Sales Director: John L. Canova
Public Relations Director: Nicholas Benton
Personnel Director: Beatrice T. Dobie
Production Director: Herbert Sorkin
Consumer Affairs Director: Carol Flaumenhaft

HOME REPAIR AND IMPROVEMENT

Editorial Staff for New Living Spaces

Editor: Philip W. Payne
Assistant Editor: Edward Brash
Picture Editor: Adrian G. Allen
Designer: Herbert H. Quarmby
Associate Designer: Anne Masters
Text Editor: Gerry Schremp
Staff Writers: Margaret Fogarty, Mary Paul,
Ted Sell, Mark M. Steele
Art Associates: Michelle Clay, Juli Hopfl, Abbe Stein,
Mary B. Wilshire, Richard Whiting
Editorial Assistant: Eleanor G. Kask

Editorial Production
Production Editor: Douglas B. Graham
Operations Manager: Gennaro C. Esposito
Assistant Production Editor: Feliciano Madrid
Quality Director: Robert L. Young
Assistant Quality Director: James J. Cox
Associate: Serafino J. Cambareri
Copy Staff: Susan B. Galloway (chief), Ricki Tarlow,
Florence Keith, Celia Beattie
Picture Department: Dolores A. Littles, Rose-Mary Hall
Traffic: Barbara Buzan

Correspondents: Elisabeth Kraemer (Bonn); Margot
Hapgood, Dorothy Bacon (London); Susan Jonas,
Lucy T. Voulgaris (New York); Maria Vincenza Aloisi,
Josephine du Brusle (Paris); Ann Natanson
(Rome). Valuable assistance was also provided by
Carolyn T. Chubet (New York).

THE CONSULTANTS: Thomas D. Ball, the general consultant for this book, is a partner in a Maryland contracting firm that specializes in home building and renovation.

Richard Ridley, architectural consultant for the book, founded an architectural firm that has won awards for urban planning and residential building. He also writes and illustrates how-to manuals to encourage his clients to participate in the design and construction of new structures.

John Drow, former chief of forest products utilization research, Forest Service, United States Department of Agriculture, is a civil engineer. He has made a number of studies of the strengths of wood and other building materials.

Harris Mitchell, special consultant for Canada, has worked in the field of home repair and improvement for more than two decades. He is editor of the magazine *Canadian Homes* and author of a syndicated newspaper column, "You Wanted to Know," as well as a number of books on home improvement.

R. Daniel Nicholson Jr., a building planner-estimator, remodels homes for customers of a Washington, D.C., home remodeling service.

John W. Hechinger is president of a chain of building-materials stores based in Washington, D.C.

Roswell W. Ard, a civil engineer, is a consulting structural engineer and a professional home inspector.

Alex Melnick is a building contractor specializing in the construction of new homes.

Contents

COLOR PORTFOLIO: A Creative Sense of Space   112

1   **New Rooms the Easy Way**   7
Ready-made Dividers—Walls That Are Not Walls   8
Partitions from Doors   10
Snap-together Modules to Enclose the Outdoors   18
Doors to Glass-in a Porch   20

2   **Putting Up and Tearing Down Walls**   27
Modern Techniques for Framing Partitions   28
Knees and Collars for an Attic   32
The Professional's Way with Wallboard   36
A Factory-fitted Door, Ready to Nail In   42
Moldings for a Neat Finish   46
Removing Walls: Simpler Than You Think   50

3   **Solid Floors and Versatile Ceilings**   59
Layered Flooring: Level, Smooth, Squeak-free   60
Custom Cuts for Borders   66
Shortcut to a Hardwood Floor   67
Building a Ceiling from Frame to Finish   68
Suspending a Ceiling   70
Putting Up a Tiled Ceiling   74

4   **Bringing In the Out-of-Doors**   81
The Trick of Converting a Window to a Door   82
A Window or Door Where There Was None   88
A Comfortable Climate in a New Living Space   102
Expanding a House by Converting a Garage   106
Transforming a Porch into a Year-round Room   114
A Labor-saving Method for Building a Deck   120

Credits and Acknowledgments   126

Index/Glossary   126

1

New Rooms the Easy Way

A versatile door. Bifold doors, bought preassembled at a hardware or building-supply store, can enclose a work or utility area or be linked together to form a movable wall as much as 8 feet wide. But they go up with less work and time than the simplest conventional wall: an overhead track and mounting brackets are installed with a single tool—a screwdriver—and even the screws are supplied by the manufacturer.

There are times when every homeowner feels a little like the old woman who lived in a shoe. Mothers trip over toddlers in cramped kitchens. Party-givers juggle food, drinks and guests between small living and dining rooms. Budding scientists and musicians compete for territory in shared bedrooms.

What these people need is new living space. Most houses contain a surprising amount of space that can be altered or adapted to a variety of family needs. Attics, garages and basements can be converted into living areas. Porches can be enclosed. Finished interior rooms can be more fully utilized—sometimes by removing walls to open up small rooms, sometimes by installing partitions that divide large rooms for disparate activities.

You can gain extra room in any of these ways, using only a few basic elements. They are standardized and relatively simple. All walls are built—or torn down—in pretty much the same way. Doors and windows come as preassembled units from a mill, ready for installation. And modern ceilings and floors are now made of factory materials specifically designed for amateurs to work with.

Even this amount of simple carpentry is not involved if you turn to "ready-mades"—prefabricated units that are used, often in ways different from their original purpose, to help you create the spaces you need. Standard shelves and cabinets, meant to provide storage, become a wall if set up freestanding to divide a large space (and they still hold books or whatever). Wide sliding or folding doors become a removable partition if hung across a large room—with the doors closed you have two small, private sections or you can conceal a work area, while opening the doors restores the large space when it is needed. It is even possible to expand the house outward with ready-mades. Rows of stock storm doors, set side-by-side and topped if necessary with a prefab aluminum roof, transform an open porch or patio into a room for all weathers.

Simple ready-mades are available at nearly all building-supply dealers. But the same techniques used in installing them apply to the much more elaborate "systems" sold in department stores and specialty shops. A customized storage unit, fitted to the available space and containing a desk, liquor cabinet, stereo—perhaps even a folding bed—can be permanently anchored employing the basic technique for setting up an inexpensive bookshelf. Folding doors that are faced with mirrors or with vivid decorator materials are hung in exactly the same way as ordinary bifold or accordion doors. Even the dramatic stainless-steel panels pictured on page 112-D are little more than sophisticated cousins of modest wooden bypass doors and are hung in virtually the same manner.

Ready-made Dividers—Walls That Are Not Walls

In rooms that serve several functions, such as traffic, work, socializing and storage, you can usually create more useful living spaces by separating the functions with various kinds of room dividers. Even the way you arrange furniture can establish walkways, work nooks and conversation areas. To create specific spaces more definitively, you can buy wood or metal frames in which to mount transparent plastic or wood or fabric-covered panels that serve essentially as screens. At greater expense, you can purchase pieces of furniture that are designed to be high enough to close off one area from another, while also functioning variously as bars, desks, storage cabinets, television-set pedestals or bookshelves.

But often you can best create your own special spaces by constructing dividers out of ready-made units intended for other purposes. Tall bookcases meant to go against a wall can be brought out to the middle of a room and made stable. You can anchor storage cabinets, including those intended for kitchens, to the floor so that they separate two areas. In a slightly more elaborate use of wall units for room division, shelving that is supported by poles running from floor to ceiling and held in place by friction can be set up in the middle of a room if secured immovably. Another solution is to install any of several kinds of folding doors that run on overhead tracks.

If you choose the kind of room divider built of bookshelves or cupboards—which are generally shallower and lighter in weight than the ready-made dividers—make sure that they will not move or topple. This can be done by fastening two units back to back (thus also hiding the unfinished parts), and by fixing them to the floor with cleats. If they are high enough, secure them to the ceiling material, which generally is strong enough to keep the divider from swaying.

Floor-to-ceiling pole-mounted shelving usually consists of wood or metal poles slotted at intervals on all four sides to receive metal shelf brackets. A spring or screw tension device, which presses the ends of the poles against floor and ceiling, holds them in place. You can use this type of shelving safely as a room divider if you balance the load on opposite sides of the pole, and secure the pole to floor and ceiling by more than simple spring pressure. Some manufacturers supply anchoring devices, but if not, you can alter the casing that encloses the spring so that you can screw it to the ceiling, and you can drill the plastic or rubber pad on which the butt rests to fasten it to the floor. If the spring casing cannot be removed, or if the pole butts against floor or ceiling, as some types do, secure the pole by confining the ends inside collars attached to floor or ceiling.

Top-hung track-mounted folding doors provide room dividers that can be removed when not needed. But, because their whole weight hangs from above, they require the most substantial installation. The tracks that support and guide the doors must be secured to the building's structure, not merely to the ceiling material, and they must be set level. To do this, build a header, attach it to the beams above the ceiling and screw the track to the bottom of it (pages 10-17).

Anchoring Storage Units

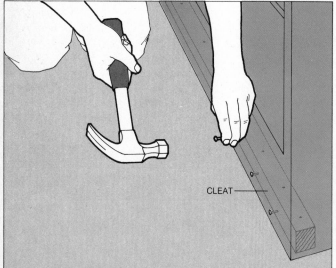

Fastening to the floor. Position the units and outline their bases in pencil. Set the units aside and draw their inside dimensions by measuring in from the outlines a distance equal to the thickness of the walls of the units. Cut two pieces of 2-by-2 to fit just inside the bottom of the unit. Nail these cleats to the floor. Set the units over the cleats and nail them together.

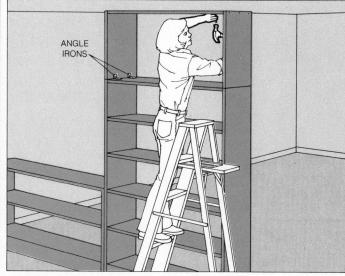

Fastening to the ceiling. Cut two pieces of 1-inch board as wide as the depth of the unit and as high as the distance between the top of the unit and the ceiling. Cut a third piece to nail between them, forming a three-sided box the length of the unit. Finish the wood as desired. Fasten the box to the unit with angle irons and attach the top of the box to the ceiling.

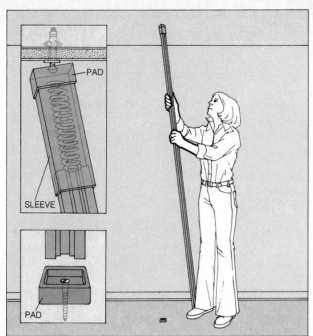

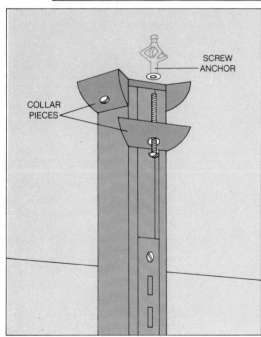

Securing Ceiling Poles

Attaching a sleeve and pad. Position the poles at 3- to 4-foot intervals. Use a level to make them vertical. Trace their ends at floor and ceiling. Dismantle the spring assembly at the end of each pole by slipping the metal sleeve and the pad seated on it away from the top of the pole (*top inset*). Bore holes through the center of the top of the pad and the sleeve, and fasten the anchor of an expansion screw in the center of the outline on the ceiling. Screw the sleeve and pad to the ceiling, but let them dangle about ⅜ inch, so that the pole can be inserted at a slight angle. Screw the pole's foot pad (*bottom inset*) to the floor. Insert the spring, compress it by pushing the top of the pole against it, and swing the pole over and into the foot pad.

Attaching a pole with collars. Miter-cut four pieces of base-shoe molding (*page 46*) to form a small frame with inside dimensions the size of the pole ends. In the center of each, and perpendicular to the face that will lie against the ceiling, bore holes the size of an expansion screw. Position the pole, hold the collar pieces against it, and mark the ceiling through the screw holes. Drill the ceiling on the marks, and expand the screw anchors in the holes. Screw the collar parts to the ceiling, tightening enough to draw the screwhead into the wood. Cover it with putty. If you use such a collar to secure the floor end of a pole, nail each part into the floor with two 1½-inch finishing nails, set and puttied.

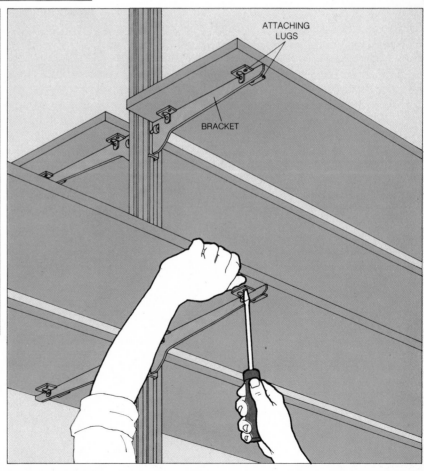

Positioning the shelves. Attach pairs of brackets to opposite sides of the poles. Lay the shelves across the brackets or screw them to the brackets through the holes in the attaching lugs (*drawing*) provided with some units.

Partitions from Doors

Folding or sliding doors hung from or guided by overhead tracks can enclose storage areas or serve as retractable walls that increase the utility of living space. These versatile barriers come in a bewildering variety of shapes, sizes and materials but can be classified generally as accordion, bifold or sliding bypass doors. The accordion and bifold types make handier room dividers than the more cumbersome sliding bypass doors, which are generally used as closet closures, but all three types can be adapted to serve as room partitions.

The accordion door looks like the bellows of an accordion and is usually made of pleated fabric or vinyl stretched over a light metal or plastic skeleton. Closing the door stretches out the pleats into a substantial-looking partition; when the door is opened, the pleats fold compactly to one side. Accordion doors, which are hung on rollers from a single overhead track and attached at one side to a wall, are the easiest of the three types of track-mounted doors to install and once in place require little or no adjustment.

Bifold doors consist of wood, plastic or metal panels up to about 2 feet wide hinged together lengthwise, usually in pairs. Pairs of panels can be linked together to form one continuous surface. A bifold door consisting of one or more pairs can be mounted at one side of an opening and closed by pulling it all the way across; or the doors can be installed at each side of an opening and pulled together at the middle. An overhead track guides the bifold door but the weight of the door rests on a pivot that is attached to the floor at the wall side. A pivot at the top of the door holds the assembly upright.

Sliding bypass doors usually consist of two large wood panels, each hung by wheels from its own overhead track. The panels overlap by about an inch and when closed are kept vertically aligned by a small floor-mounted guide. All overhead tracks—whether they support or merely guide a door—sustain considerable stress when the doors are in use and should be attached to a level, structurally supported surface.

Occasionally a track can be fastened directly to the ceiling. But since folding or sliding doors more than 6 feet 8 inches high are seldom readily available and since most ceilings are around 8 feet high, installing such doors usually involves attaching the track for the door to a header suspended from the joists, the structural beams that support the ceiling and the floor above.

The location of the joists helps to determine the position of the door. After locating the joists and marking the proposed position of the door, carefully calculate the vertical space needed for the door and its track. Design and construct a header suitable for the type of ceiling involved to fit in the space between the track and the ceiling.

To calculate the height of header to be suspended from a permanently attached ceiling, measure from floor to ceiling at several points along the proposed line of the door. Subtract from the shortest of these measurements (thus allowing for any unevenness in the floor or ceiling) the height of the door and its track plus the thickness of the wallboard or other covering to be applied to the bottom of the header. The result is the height of the header frame; its length is the distance from wall to wall. Attach the header to the ceiling joists, fasten the track to the header and mount the door in its track.

For a door that is hung directly from the ceiling, locate the joists and attach the track directly to them through the ceiling material.

Positioning the Door

1 **Locating the joists.** To locate joists concealed by a permanently attached ceiling, drill a small hole through the ceiling and probe through the hole with a stiff wire to determine the location of the nearest joist and the direction in which it runs. Since joists are usually placed parallel to each other across the narrow dimension of a house with their centers 16 inches apart, the location of one joist discloses the locations of others. The header for a door mounted parallel to the run of the joists will be attached all along its length to a single joist. To determine the exact location of this joist you may have to probe at two widely separated points. For a header that runs parallel to, but between, two joists, construct the same type of subceiling as for an interior partition in the same position (*pages 28-29*).

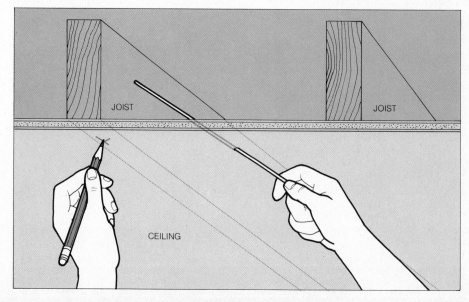

2 **Marking the position of the door.** Use a chalk line to mark the location of the header. Unreel the chalk-covered line from its housing, hold or fasten it taut across the ceiling from wall to wall along the line to be marked and snap it like a bowstring, leaving a straight, sharp chalk mark across the ceiling. If this line runs at right angles to the joists, mark the position of each joist. These marks, placed a little to one side of the chalk mark, will guide you later in attaching the header. Make a vertical chalk mark down the wall at each end of the chalk mark across the ceiling. To make sure the line is vertical, hang a plumb bob at the end of the chalk line, then secure and snap the line. These vertical lines will guide you later in attaching a header frame and attaching and aligning doors.

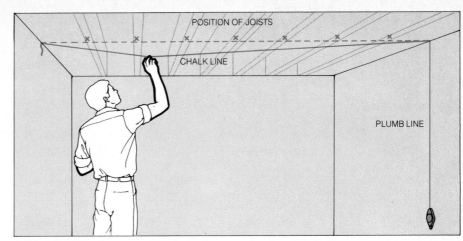

Hanging a Header

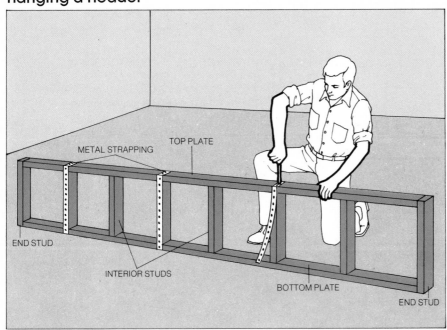

1 **Constructing the header.** Build a frame like the one for a nonbearing partition wall (pages 28-31), using 2-by-4s and 16-penny common nails. Cut the two end vertical studs to the exact height of the frame and butt-nail the top and bottom plates between them to form a rectangular box. Fill in the box with interior vertical studs nailed 16 inches apart. If the header is to be mounted perpendicular, rather than parallel, to the run of the joists, the first of these interior studs should be nailed 8 inches from one end of the frame studs and 16 inches apart thereafter so that they will not fall directly beneath joists. Reinforce the frame by attaching perforated metal strapping over the top plate and down the sides of every other interior stud.

2 **Attaching and leveling the header.** While a helper holds the frame in place, using the wall and ceiling chalk marks as guides, fasten the sides of the frame to the walls with nails driven partway. Check the frame with a carpenter's level.

3 **Shimming the frame.** If necessary, level the frame by shimming, i.e., driving thin wood wedges between the top plate and the ceiling. A good shimming technique is to drive in segments of cedar shingle from opposite sides of the top plate to form a tight rectangular block.

4 **Securing the frame.** Once the frame is level, nail or screw it firmly into the joists. For extra security, screw the frame to the joists every 2 feet or so with ¼-inch lag bolts. Trim off the shims flush with the frame. Finish the frame with wallboard or paneling (*pages 36-41*).

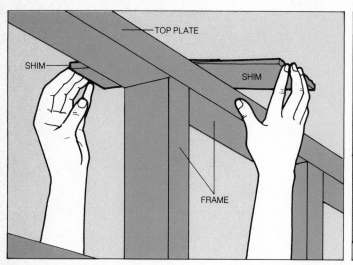

TOP PLATE

SHIM

SHIM

FRAME

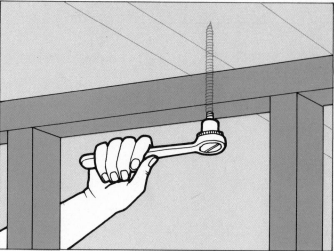

A Header for a Suspended Ceiling: Between Joists

1 **Installing supports.** To make supports for a header that runs parallel to the joists above a suspended ceiling, cut lengths of 2-by-4 to fit between two adjoining joists. The header can now be suspended from these supports with lengths of a continuously threaded metal rod. With a wood bit ¹⁄₁₆ inch or so larger than the diameter of the rod, drill a hole through the broad side of each support at its center. Nail the supports between the two joists at intervals of about 2 feet with their broad sides flush with the bottom edges of the joists.

CEILING FRAMEWORK

2 **Attaching the header.** Cut segments of rod to a length equal to the distance from the tops of the supports to the level of the ceiling plus about 3 inches. Insert a length of rod through each support, sandwiching it with two nuts, a washer under the top nut; allow the rods to protrude about 2 inches below the ceiling.

Cut a 2-by-4 the length of the proposed track. Hold it in position, broad side up, and mark the location of each rod. Drill countersink holes at these points with a spade bit the size of the washers you will use. Then drill holes through the header the same size as those in the supports. Attach the header, its countersunk holes down, to the rods, sandwiching it between two nuts on each rod, a washer above the bottom nut. Adjust the nuts on each rod until the top of the header is flush with the ceiling and no rod protrudes from the bottom of the header.

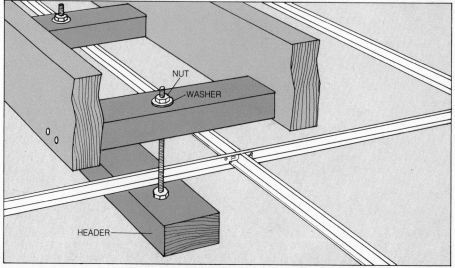

NUT

WASHER

HEADER

A Header for a Suspended Ceiling: Across Joists

1 **Preparing the support and header.** Cut two 2-by-4s the length of the opening. Remove the cross Ts from the ceiling frame along the line proposed for the door. Hold one of the 2-by-4s up to the joists along this line and mark points about 2 feet apart at which you can insert threaded rod through this support without encountering joists, pipes, ducts or the framework of the ceiling. Drill holes for rods through both of the 2-by-4s as in Step 2, at left.

2 **Installing the support and the header.** Attach the support 2-by-4 to the bottom edges of the joists along the proposed line of the door. For a heavy door, attach the support to every other joist with ¼-inch lag bolts. Connect the header to the support with lengths of rod and level the header, as in Step 2, at left.

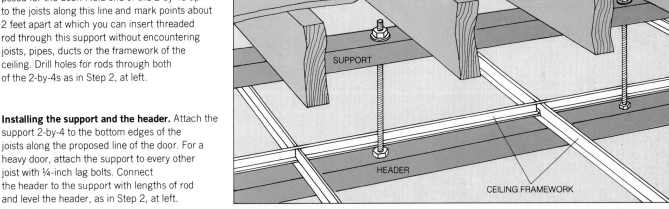

3 **Trimming and replacing ceiling panels.** Align each panel in turn with its space in the grid. Mark on each panel the position of the protruding rod. If the header runs alongside a grid member (*right*), notch each panel to accommodate the rod and replace the panel. If the header runs between two grid members, cut the panels in two where the header divides them. Notch each of the panels to accommodate the rods and replace them with the notches above the header.

Installing an Accordion Door

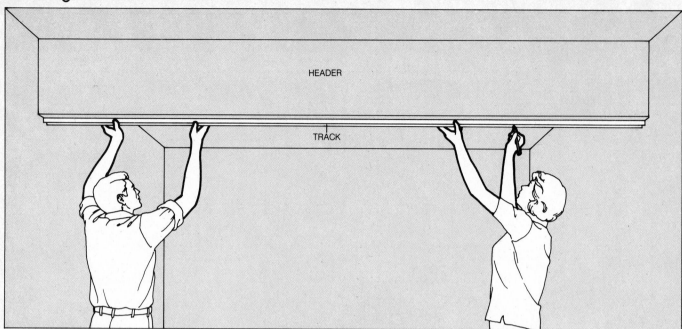

1 **Positioning the track.** Place the track on the header and mark the screw holes. Remove the track and make starter holes for the screws.

2 **Attaching the door to the track.** Without re-moving the tape or cardboard bands that hold the door in its stacked position, slip the rollers at the top of the door into the track.

3 **Mounting the door.** Stand the entire assembly beneath the header with the door at one end of the track. Attach the other end of the track to the header. Slide the door to the fastened end of the track and attach the rest of the track.

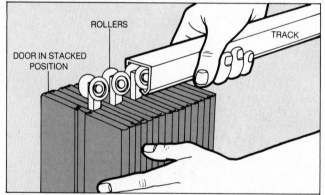

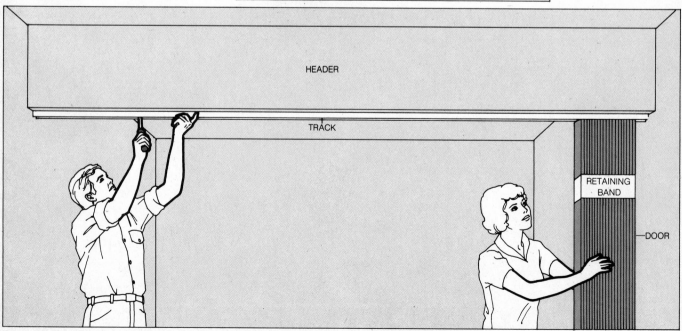

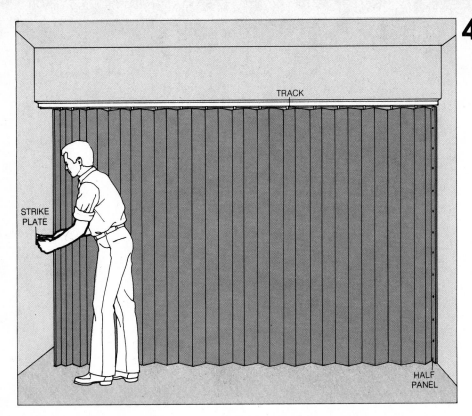

4 **Positioning the strike plate.** Drop a plumb line from the center of the track along the wall to which you will attach one side of the door. Along this vertical line, attach the door's wall panel, which is usually a hinged half panel with holes predrilled for mounting. Extend the door to the opposite wall. Position the strike plate into which the door latch will fit. Align the strike plate horizontally with the latch and vertically with the center of the track and attach it to the wall.

Installing Bifold Doors

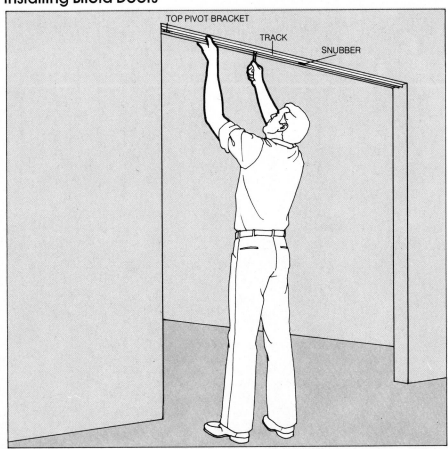

1 **Mounting track and top brackets.** Before attaching the track of a bifold door to the header, insert into the track the bracket that holds the pivot for the top of the door and the rubber or plastic snubber that cushions the impact of the door as it closes. When mounting doors on each side of an opening, insert a top pivot bracket at each end of the track with a snubber between them. Then attach the track.

2 **Mounting the bottom pivot bracket.** Slide the top pivot bracket against the wall. Drop a plumb line from the center of the bracket to the floor. Position the bottom pivot bracket directly beneath the top bracket. Screw the bottom bracket to the wall and to the floor. To provide clearance between the bottom of the door and a carpet, mount the bracket on a small wood block *(inset)* the thickness of the carpet.

3 **Mounting and positioning the door.** With the door panels folded together, slip the door's bottom pivot into the bottom pivot socket. Slide the top pivot bracket toward the center of the track and position the door under it. Slip the top pivot socket over the top pivot. As you push the top pivot bracket and the door back toward the wall, slip the spring-mounted slide guide at the top of the door into the track.

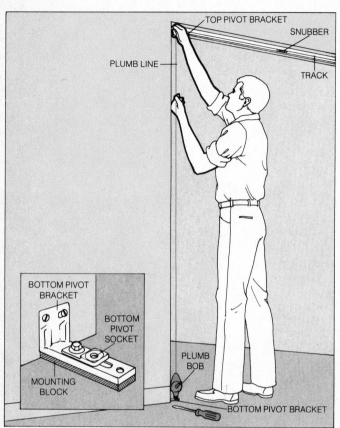

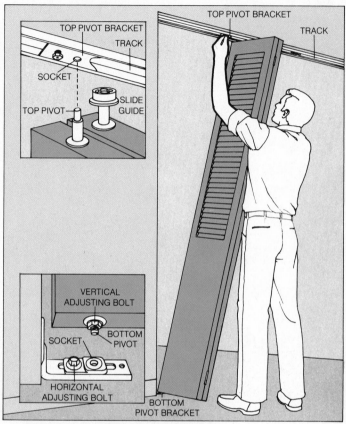

4 **Adjusting the door.** Most manufacturers supply with each door a wrench made to fit the bolts that lock the bottom and top pivot sockets in place. Loosen these bolts, adjust the pivot sockets horizontally until the door extends and folds properly, then tighten the bolts. The door may be raised or lowered slightly by turning the vertical adjusting bolt on the door's bottom pivot.

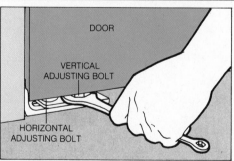

5 **Mounting the aligners.** Bifold doors mounted on each side of an opening and meeting in the middle when closed are usually held flush and in line with metal aligners. Close the doors and mount one aligner on the back of each door.

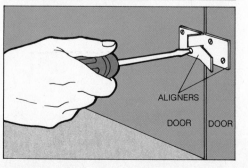

Installing Sliding Doors

1 Hanging the doors. The track for a pair of top-hung bypass sliding doors has two parallel channels. Each door is hung from carriers whose wheels fit into these channels. Proper operation of the doors demands a level header on which to mount the track and careful measurements for the doors themselves. Order sliding doors the height of the opening less 1¾ inches: 1½-inch clearance at the top for the track, ¼ inch at the floor. In width, each door should measure one half the opening plus ½ inch, to allow a 1-inch overlap when the doors are closed.

Attach the track to the header with the open sides of the two channels toward the rear of the closet or other area that the doors will enclose. Hang the innermost door first. Face the closed side of the track. Holding the door with the top tilted away from you, hook the carrier wheels into the rear channel. Hang the other door from the front channel in the same way.

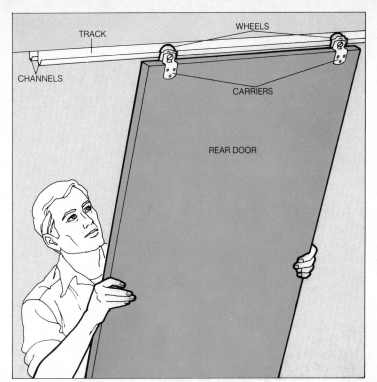

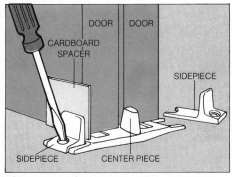

2 Attaching the floor guide. A small two-channeled plastic or metal device fastened to the floor at the center of the opening helps keep the doors aligned and prevents them from swaying laterally as they slide. A common type of aligner is the adjustable three-piece design shown above. To fasten it, hold the doors plumb and insert the center portion of the floor guide between them and attach it to the floor. With the doors hanging free, use a piece of cardboard as a spacer to position each of the two sidepieces about 1⁄16 inch from the outside of each door. Fasten the sidepieces to the floor.

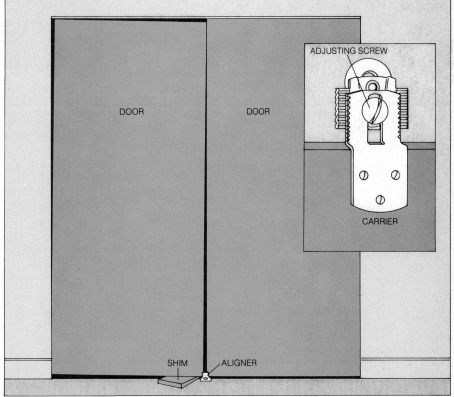

3 Aligning the doors. If the edge of a door does not meet the wall squarely, loosen the adjusting screws on the carriers, push shims between the bottom of the door and the floor until the door squares with the wall, then tighten the screws.

Snap-together Modules to Enclose the Outdoors

Ready-mades, so useful for remodeling a home's interior, have counterparts for extending living space out of doors. Handiest of these are aluminum roofing panels, which can be used to shade a patio or driveway, and aluminum wall panels *(pages 20-25),* which can be used to enclose an outdoor living space.

Such panels fit together on ready-made frames. Pieces snap into one another and minor adjustments can be made by simply sliding components around before fastening them with screws—of aluminum or stainless steel to prevent corrosion. The materials are easy to handle and practically maintenance-free.

Roofing panels, called pans because of their U-shaped contours, are locked in place by a four-sided frame of special-ized channels, called fascias. End fascias, which hold the ends of the pans, are supported along one edge by the wall of the house and along the opposite edge by posts; support is provided at the house end of the roof by mounting the end fascia on the wall. The two end fascias include troughs that act as gutters to carry away water. Two lengths of side fascia complete the frame and help the roof resist wind stress.

To erect a patio or carport roof, first determine how large it will be and the height at which it will project from the house. It should be the same size or slightly smaller than the slab over which it will project; if it is to project more than 12 feet from the house you will need professional guidance.

Supporting posts should be tall enough so the roof clears any windows or doors in the house wall. If the covered patio is to be enclosed, the roof should be no more than 89 inches above the slab; otherwise, special oversized enclosure panels will be needed. Also, square aluminum posts secured with L-shaped straps should be substituted for the decorative supports and post fittings shown here; the square posts afford the flat surfaces needed to install the wall panels.

Once these size and style decisions have been made, parts can be ordered to size, often in kit form, from a building-supplies dealer. Downspouts, also available in kit form, come in a variety of types to match the gutter systems built into the roof frames.

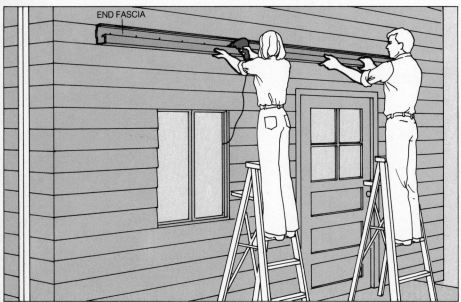

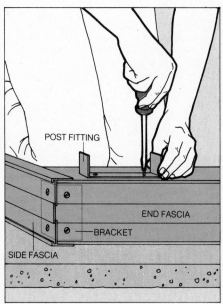

1 Mounting the end fascia. Snap a chalk line on the house wall at the height of the support posts and check the line with a level. (If the patio is not sloped away from the house for drainage, make the line an inch higher to give the roof a slight pitch.) For a house with wood or aluminum siding, locate the studs, using the joist-finding technique shown on page 10, and draw vertical lines at the points where they intersect the chalk line. With a helper, hold one strip of end fascia against the house, its bottom on the chalk line; drill pilot holes through the fascia and siding into the studs at each marked point and insert 3-inch wood screws. If the siding is not flat, such as with a clapboard house, put shims—wedge-shaped wood shingles—behind the fascia to plumb it before finally tightening the screws.

For a brick house, drill through the fascia where it crosses every other vertical mortar joint, pushing the drill just far enough to mark the mortar. Put the fascia aside and use a ½-inch masonry bit to drill into the mortar joints. Tap in ¼-inch lead anchors. Secure the fascia to the wall by driving 1¼-inch, No. 8 screws into the anchors. Caulk along the joint between the top of the fascia and the wall.

2 Preparing the end and side fascias. For an open patio or carport, lap the second piece of end fascia over the short bracket mounted at the end of one side fascia, aligning the two at the corner. Drill two pilot holes through the end fascia and fasten the pieces together with ⅜-inch sheet-metal screws. Set a post fitting on the underside of the end fascia approximately 1 inch from the corner and secure it with a pair of sheet-metal screws. Similarly mount a second post fitting at the other end of the end fascia. If the end fascia is more than 12 feet long, mount a fitting for a third post midway between the corner posts. For an enclosed patio, attach short pieces of L angle *(page 23, Step 1)* rather than post fittings.

3 **Raising the fascia frame.** To make temporary braces for the roof frame, first nail 2-by-4 crosspieces, each 12 inches long, 3 inches from the ends of four 10-foot 2-by-4s. Finish each brace with a second, shorter piece nailed across the first one (inset) to form a two-pronged fork. With a helper and the temporary braces, raise the screwed-together side and end fascias into place. Drill pilot holes and screw the free end of the side piece to the fascia already mounted on the house. At the other side, lay a 1-by-4 over the two pieces of end fascia, an inch from their outside edges, and screw it down with 1-inch screws to serve as additional temporary bracing. Slip the support posts up under their fittings and fasten with sheet-metal screws.

4 **Assembling the roof.** Slide a roof pan into the end fascia channels at the open side of the frame, keeping the lips at the top of the pan toward you. Push the pan through the channels and fasten it to the top lip of the side fascia, installing sheet-metal screws every 12 inches. Slide a second pan into the channels; bend the far wall of the second pan forward, slip it under the lip of the first pan and release it so the two lips lock together (inset). Slide the pans in and lock them together until all pans are in place. Attach the remaining piece of side fascia and pull the last pan toward it (the pans will bend sufficiently to give some play); secure the last pan to the side fascia with sheet-metal screws.

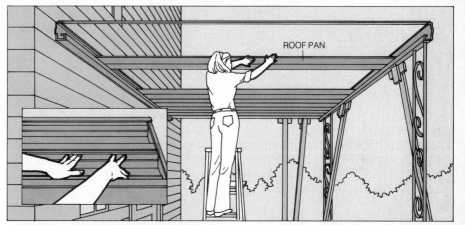

5 **Fitting the support posts.** Plumb each support post with the aid of a level and mark where its legs meet the patio or driveway. Move the post out of the way. Drill two holes through a post fitting, center it over the floor markings and mark hole positions on the slab. For a concrete slab, remove the fitting and drill a pair of ½-inch holes into the slab, tap in ¼-inch lead anchors, replace the fitting and screw it into place.

For a wood deck, use 1-inch wood screws to secure the fittings. Slip the post over the fitting and secure it with two sheet-metal screws.

Remove all the temporary bracing. Insert two sheet-metal screws through the bottoms of both ends of each pan into the end channels to anchor the pans in place. Caution: do not walk on the pans; instead lift a sheet of plywood onto the roof to support yourself while you secure the pan ends nearest the house. Follow the manufacturer's instructions to install the downspouts.

Doors to Glass-in a Porch

Aluminum storm doors ordered without the usual hinges or handles can serve as weatherproof wall panels to turn a roofed patio, porch or breezeway into a protected sunroom. (Converting a porch into a full-fledged room is a more complicated undertaking, as shown on pages 114-119.) Any storm door can be adapted for enclosing a sunroom, but three are especially popular. For areas where the weather tends to be fickle, a good choice is a self-storing panel, with permanent screens and sliding glass panes.

Equally versatile are screened jalousie panels, which can be cranked shut in a flash against a sudden sprinkle; while they are somewhat more expensive than self-storing panels, they allow for greater areas of open screening and thus more air circulation on pleasant days.

For regions with relatively constant weather, single-view panels serve well; they consist of a frame and a large piece of interchangeable glass or screen—but the glass has to be removed and stored while the screens are in use. They are not recommended for families with young children, since the glass extends almost all the way to the floor and can be a safety hazard to an errant tricyclist.

All three sorts of panels—plus the attendant hardware—are readily available in aluminum finish or white; some manufacturers also offer a variety of baked-on enamel colors.

While panels are available in virtually any width, those less than 40 inches wide are easier to handle and sturdier than larger ones. Heights normally range up to 89 inches. For porches taller than 89 inches, oversized panels can be ordered or aluminum and glass transoms can be added above each panel to fill up the space. (If the porch is gabled, the triangular opening between the roof support and the roof is closed by nailing up siding or exterior-grade plywood sheathing.)

The first crucial step in enclosing a porch is to outline and measure, with the aid of chalk lines and a plumb bob, each wall opening—that is, each space between existing posts, or between a post and the side of the house. Once the vertical and horizontal dimensions of each wall opening have been determined, you can quickly calculate the size of all the needed components by following the formulas described in Steps 2 and 3 on these pages and—if the prospective wall will have a door—making the additional adjustments explained overleaf. Most porches are sloped for drainage, but you will not have to buy different-sized panels to compensate for the incline of the floor; wherever the walls need to be slightly taller, the panels can simply be raised within the 2-inch-deep channel that secures their base.

Doors can be positioned anywhere in an enclosure wall, but they require advance planning at the time that basic panel sizes are being calculated. Operating doors can be the same style as the wall panels or they can contrast.

When installation is complete, dab a bit of caulking along the base of the wall and into any small gaps where panels meet the side of the house. With these last protective touches, the glass will keep out chilly winds and will trap the sun's heat to extend the use of a patio room several weeks into cooler seasons. And in the summer, with the screens in place, the room will be cool, airy and pleasantly bug-free.

A finished wall. An enclosure wall consists of panels held in place by two kinds of aluminum channel, F channel and H channel—so called because of the shapes of their cross sections. The tops and bottoms of the panels are anchored with F channel that fastens into the patio floor and into the roof support. The sides of the wall are held in place by F channel fastened to posts or the side of the house; these side F channels stand on top of the base F channel and also butt against the bottom edge of the top F channel (inset, bottom left). The H channel joins adjacent panels; it stands on top of the base F channel and pushes halfway up into the top F channel (insets, top and bottom right).

All channels are fastened to the panels with $\frac{3}{8}$-inch No. 6 stainless-steel sheet-metal screws. Side and top channels are anchored into wood posts, siding or roof supports with aluminum wood screws, or into concrete and brick with masonry pin-grip fasteners (page 22).

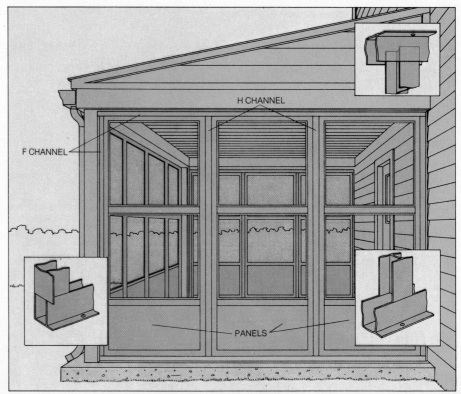

H CHANNEL

F CHANNEL

PANELS

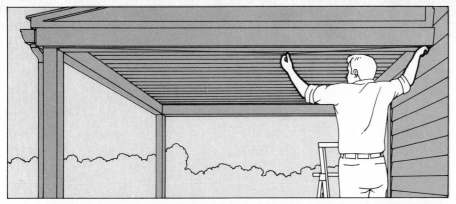

Aligning the Enclosure

1 **Marking the top of a wall.** Tack one end of a chalk line into the underside of the roof support, flush with the outer edge of a corner post. Hold the opposite end of the chalk line the same distance in from the edge of the roof support —either at another post or against the side of the house, as here—and snap it to establish the position of the outer edge of the top of the wall.

2 **Marking and measuring a base line.** Hold a plumb line at several points along the top line and have a helper mark where the plumb bob touches the floor. Connect these marks with a chalk line or straightedge to establish the position for the outer edge of the bottom of the wall. Measure the top and base lines to determine the lengths of the F channels that will be needed to hold the top and bottom of the wall in place. Next, to determine the width of the panels, divide the base-line length into as many segments as necessary to achieve convenient-sized, matching panels—and then subtract 1 inch from the width of each panel to allow room for sections of H channel that will fit between them.

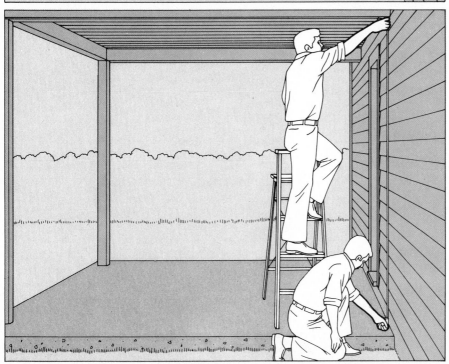

3 **Height measurements.** If the porch floor or patio is not sloped slightly away from the house for drainage, a single measurement of the floor-to-ceiling height can be used to calculate the height of panels and the size of H channels and vertical F channels. To figure the height of the panels, subtract ¼ inch from the floor-to-ceiling height; this allows room for the top and bottom F channels. To figure the size of the H channels that will fit between adjacent panels mid-wall, subtract 3 inches from the height; this permits the H channels to sit on top of the base F channel and push halfway up into the top F channel. To figure the size of the two side F channels, subtract 4 inches from the height; this allows the vertical F channels to sit on top of the F channel along the floor and to fit underneath the F channel that spans the top of the opening.

If the base is sloped, the height of all the panels should be equal to the shortest floor-to-ceiling height (usually at the side of the house), minus ¼ inch. Separate measurements for H channels should be made at each point where panels will join, and the height of each side of the opening must be separately measured for the vertical F channels at the ends of the wall.

Assembling the Door Panels

1 Attaching the base F channel. Place the edge of the base F-channel flange along the chalk line, with the flange facing the outside. Drill every 24 inches through the flange and into the floor. If the floor is wood, screw the channel down with ½-inch screws, if concrete use masonry pin-grip fasteners—combination nail-and-expansion bolts. Slip each fastener into a hole and then hammer home the pin on top. This forces the bottom of the fastener's stem to spread out, holding it securely in the concrete (*insets, below*).

2 Assembling the wall. Remove the glass from the panels for easier handling and lay the panels out on the porch floor in the order they will take in the finished wall. Slip the side F channels onto the sides of the outer panels. Slip the edge of each panel into its H channel. Adjust all channels so their lower ends are 2 inches above the bottoms of the panels, which will later be slipped into the base F channel. Slip the upper F channel over the top of the whole assembly, pushing it over the outsides of the H channels.

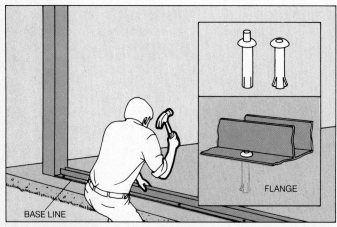

BASE LINE

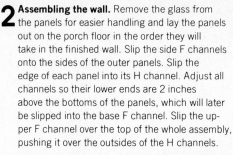

FLANGE

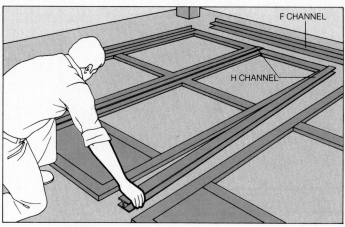

F CHANNEL

H CHANNEL

KICK PLATE

3 Raising the wall. With a helper, slip the bottoms of the panels into the base F channel and raise the wall into position. Every 24 inches, fasten the flanges of the side and top F channels into the corner posts, the roof frame and the house wall. Use ½-inch round-head wood screws for wood posts, roof frames and house siding. If the roof frame is aluminum, use ⅜-inch sheet-metal screws. If the house is brick, secure the side F channel with masonry pin-grip fasteners placed in the mortar between bricks. After the wall is secured, slide panels left or right so that each one extends approximately the same distance into the vertical F and H channels.

4 Aligning the panels. Although porch floors often slope slightly away from a house for drainage, panels should be even all along the length of a wall. Starting at the highest point on the floor, usually next to the house, push the first panel all the way down into the base F channel. Secure this panel by drilling pilot holes every 24 inches along the side channels and inserting sheet-metal screws. Also, insert two screws each through the top and bottom F channels.

Raise the adjacent panel until the top of its kick plate is level with the kick plate of the first panel. You may need a helper to hold the panel while you screw it into place. Working along the wall, adjust each panel to the same level and screw it into place. Replace all the panel glass.

Providing an Entrance

If a door is needed in any of the walls of the porch enclosure, its installation will call for several additional sorts of supporting hardware. The largest of these are lengths of 2-by-2 aluminum to serve as framing posts and as the header—the crosswise piece at the top of the frame. You will also require two descriptively named components—a Z bar and an L angle. The former is equipped with a rubber or vinyl gasket and provides a weather seal between the door and the frame. The L angle *(Step 1, right)* serves to hold the doorposts and the header in place. Use an L angle with 1½-inch legs.

If the door opening is taller than 80 inches, the door should have a transom over it; tall doors are hard to open and close and tend to bend out of shape over the years. Also, doors should be at least 36 inches wide to allow furniture to be moved in and out.

The presence of a door naturally affects the construction of the rest of a wall. Spaces at either side of the door will be treated as separate wall openings for the measurements needed to order panels and supporting channels *(page 21, Steps 2 and 3)*. If the door can be located in such a way that equal-width panels can fill out the two sides, so much the better. But sometimes a walkway or existing steps dictate a door's placement. In that case, panels of two different widths can be used at either side of the door, or the panel width may be kept uniform—except for a narrow side panel used at one end of a wall to fill in an odd space. When calculating the sizes of wall components, remember to allow for both the width of the door and the 2-inch post on each side of it.

A similar caution applies when figuring the height of the door (or door plus transom). Be sure to subtract 2 inches from the height of the opening for the 2-inch header, another $\frac{1}{16}$ inch for clearance between the door and header, and ½ inch for clearance at the bottom of the door. (A ½-inch vinyl sweep will keep air from pouring in under the door.)

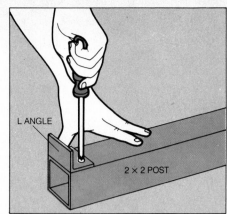

1 Preparing side posts. A short piece of L angle—2 inches long or slightly less—will have to be mounted on each end of both doorposts so the posts can be anchored to the floor and the roof support. Drill two pilot holes through one side of the L angles and into the posts, and use ⅜-inch sheet-metal screws to attach the L angles.

2 Erecting the hinge-side post. Use two screws to fasten the L angle at the top of one post to the roof support at the point planned for the hinge side of the door. The L angle should extend toward the outside of the porch and its outer edge should touch the top line. Next, tack a plumb line to the roof support near the post and adjust the position of the bottom of the post for verticality, using the plumb line and bottom chalk line as guides. Fasten the bottom L angle in place, using masonry pin-grip fasteners if the floor is concrete, screws if it is wood.

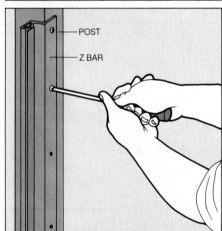

3 Installing a Z bar. Mount a piece of Z bar along the hinge-side post as shown, drilling pilot holes and placing sheet-metal screws every 24 inches. Since the door will have ½-inch clearance at the bottom, the Z bar should be as long as the height of the door plus ½ inch.

4 Hanging the door. Have a helper hold the door in place, using scrap as a support. The door should clear the floor by about ½ inch. If the header will be installed against the roof frame *(page 24, Step 7)*, be sure to position the door to leave a $\frac{1}{16}$-inch clearance at the top. Lay the free hinge leaf against the Z bar and mark screw positions on the Z bar through the predrilled holes in the hinge leaf. Drill pilot holes through the Z bar and into the post, and screw the hinge in with sheet-metal screws.

5 **Erecting the strike-side post.** Install a Z bar, as described in Step 3 on page 23. Then have a helper hold the post in position—allowing 1/16-inch clearance between the door and frame—and screw the top and bottom L angles into place.

6 **Notching the Z bar.** Sometimes the Z bar bought with a storm door will be notched for fitting across the top of the door. If not, use a hacksaw to cut away a piece of the metal and gasket so that the Z bar will butt properly with the two side Z bars. Screw the notched Z bar to the underside of the header before the header is installed.

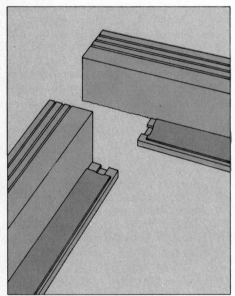

7 **Installing the header.** If the header is to mount directly under the roof support (*right*), mount an L angle along one of its surfaces with sheet-metal screws. Use wood screws at 8-inch intervals to screw the L angle into the support.

If the header is to be positioned lower to allow room for a transom (*far right*), it will hang from short pieces of L angle first attached to the side posts. The L angle will protrude into the header, which will conceal it. Attach one leg of the L angle to each side post; the top of the protruding leg should be 1/16 inch below where the top of the header is to be. Slip one end of the header onto a protruding leg. Then push the side posts outward—they are flexible enough to move without becoming permanently bent—and slip the second end of the header onto the L angle. Drill pilot holes through the top of the header into the L angle, and fasten with sheet-metal screws.

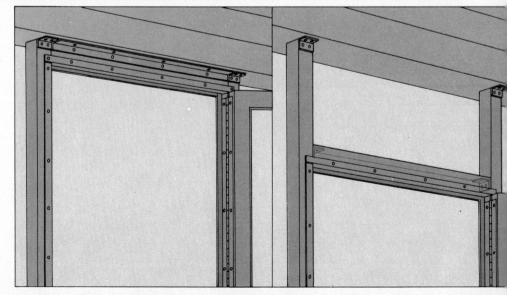

Installing a Transom

1 **Framing a transom.** A frame into which a transom panel can be screwed is formed by long pieces of L angle attached to the top side of the header, the doorposts and the underside of the roof support. Mount the side pieces of L angle with sheet-metal screws at 8-inch intervals. Notch the top and bottom pieces of the L angle *(inset)* and screw them into place.

2 **Installing the transom.** Holding the transom in place, drill two pilot holes through each side piece of the L-angle frame and into the metal frame of the transom. Anchor the transom in place with sheet-metal screws.

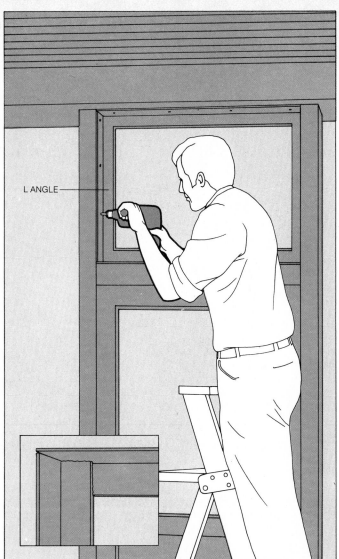

L ANGLE

Extenders for Odd Sizes

If your floor-to-ceiling opening is greater than 89 inches (the maximum normal height of panels), you may want to put a transom over each panel rather than ordering oversized doors. When figuring the height of your panels and transoms, subtract ¾ inch from the height of the opening to allow room for the horizontal crosspiece of H channel that will join the top of the panel and the bottom of the transom. When assembling the wall, slip the ends of the H channel into the vertical F or H channels that hold each panel in place. Slip the transom into position and erect and secure the wall.

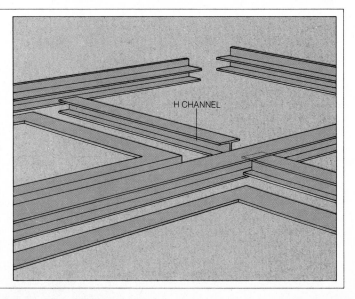

H CHANNEL

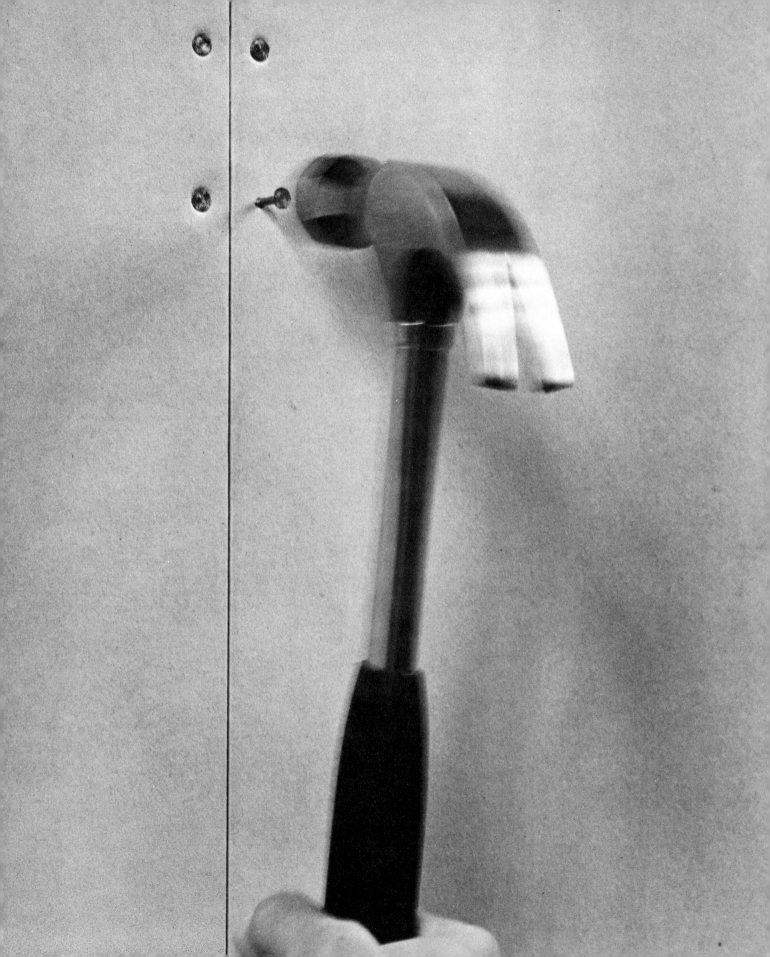

2

Putting Up and Tearing Down Walls

Double insurance. The studs that hold wallboard expand and contract as the house settles and temperature changes. Putting in the nails two by two reinforces their holding power so they are less likely to pop out than single nails. Driving nails in a fraction of an inch below the surface of the wallboard with the last hammer blow insets them so they can be concealed with joint compound to give the wallboard a smooth finish.

Nothing transforms the interior of a house more dramatically than adding new walls or taking out old ones. Partitioning a living room can create an attractive front hall where none exists or turn a dining alcove into a full-fledged room. Demolishing a partition can expand a living room by combining it with a little-used den. In many old homes, an invitingly spacious living room can be created by removing the partition or doorway that separates parlor from dining room.

Putting up—or removing—a wall is considerably simpler than most people imagine. The reason is the standardized construction that has been used for several decades. Nearly all home walls consist of a framework of vertical and horizontal 2-by-4s sandwiched between sheets of wallboard. When you are adding such a wall, you construct the frame on the floor, where you can work comfortably; then you attach a nailing plate to the floor and hang the frame above it like a huge wooden curtain *(pages 28-31)*. Providing a door is a simple matter of leaving an opening in the frame and installing a prehung unit *(pages 42-45)* after you finish the wall.

Subtracting walls involves one additional consideration because some are bearing walls, that is, they carry part of the weight of the house. Nonbearing walls can be treated as dispensable; they come out slick as a whistle. Bearing walls, however, must be replaced with supporting beams that will always remain visible *(pages 50-57)*.

All permanent partitions attach to joists and studs, and many of them hold electric wires, heating ducts, even plumbing pipes. Before you launch into adding or subtracting walls, analyze your house carefully. If you are lucky enough to have construction drawings on hand, you can get some clues from them, but do not rely on them—they do not normally show all details of framing, piping and wiring, and the details they show were very likely followed only partly by the builders. You can get the information you need with a little detective work. Tapping ceiling and walls helps indicate basic construction, but the only sure way to learn what is where is to make small holes so that you can look inside the walls.

Before moving partitions, study family traffic patterns to avoid turning the main floor into an obstacle course or placing a door where it will block a window. Note the directions that windows face in, so you can preserve cross ventilation and natural lighting. If you have trouble visualizing the effect a new wall will have, approximate it roughly by hanging sheets from the ceiling and consider the effect for awhile. If your plans call for removing a wall, a dry run will be impossible and you will have to rely on accurate measurements and scale drawings to show how the space will change and how your furniture will fit into the new interior arrangement.

Modern Techniques for Framing Partitions

Building a wall to divide an existing space is rather like hanging a curtain—a curtain made of wood. Like a curtain, the frame of the new wall goes into place not from the floor up, but from the ceiling down. Only in the last stage of assembly is it fastened to the floor.

In the simplest building methods, shown on these pages, most of the frame is assembled flat on the floor. It is lifted as a unit over a beam called a sole plate that is nailed to the floor. Once upright, the wall frame is fastened in place by nails driven through a second beam, called a top plate, into the joists hidden above the ceiling. Finally, the bottom of the assembly is secured by nails driven through the sole plate.

For this final step, in which vertical beams called studs are nailed to the horizontal sole plate, you must master the knack of toenailing—that is, of fastening two pieces of lumber together at a right angle by driving a nail through them at an angle of about 45°. Toenailing a stud to a plate is easy after some practice, but at the beginning you may prefer to make a path for the toenails by drilling diagonal starter holes downward through the stud and into the plate, using a bit slightly smaller than the nail.

Ideally, the new wall should run either across the ceiling joists or under a single joist, so that the top plate can be nailed directly into a beam or beams above it.

Ideally, too, the outermost stud of the new wall should lie directly against a stud in the existing wall, for easy stud-to-stud fastening. These ideal placements are not always practical. When you must run a wall between joists or end it between studs, you will have to install short lengths of wood as nailing blocks between the joists or studs (opposite, Step 3) to support it.

Sometimes age and traffic will have caused the ceiling or the floor joists to sag. In these cases, you may have to insert shims—short lengths of thin wood—between the top plate and the ceiling or between the sole plate and the floor to make sure that a plate is level and firm before nailing it in place.

The other decisions you must make will affect the interior and the sheathing of the wall frame. One has to do with electrical outlets. You can install them easily in the open frame before the wallboard is nailed on and place them wherever you please. Usually, power for the new outlets can be taken from an existing outlet box in a nearby house circuit. Turn off the power to the circuit and make connections from the hot, neutral and ground wires in the existing box to the corresponding wires of a plastic-sheathed cable, using wire nuts (page 73). Then run the cable through holes drilled through the new wall studs to new outlet boxes installed on the studs

(page 31, Step 9), secure the cable inside the boxes with clamps and strip the ends of the cable wires. Do not install new outlets back-to-back: the arrangement is common when new wiring is installed in walls because it reduces the need for wall patching after the installation, but back-to-back outlets can increase sound-carrying problems in a house.

Sound suppression is even more important when you choose the sheathing for the new wall. The thickness of this sheathing directly affects the transmission of sound from one room to another. For example, gypsum wallboard that is ⅝ inch—rather than the standard thickness, ½ inch—will cut sound transmission through a wall by more than 15 per cent. The extra cost of the thicker board may well seem worthwhile: it reduces the sound of a conversation in the next room—in the language of acoustical engineers—from "audible and intelligible" to "audible but not intelligible."

Installing doors in a new wall is a separate operation, treated on pages 34-35 and 42-43: a door is built as a package with its own framing system, and the entire unit fits into a standard wall. But the placement of a door must be decided in advance. Choose the spot with care, with an eye to the traffic patterns of the new room, its planned decor and the fact that an open door should not cover a window or a light switch.

A Wall Built on the Floor, Tilted into Place

1 **Marking the top and sole plates.** Measure the length of the ceiling across which the new wall will run and cut two 2-by-4s to this length for the top and sole plates. On the top plate mark off areas 1½ inches wide for studs, one at each end and the others with their centers either 16 or 24 inches apart, depending on local building codes. Standard wallboard panels conform to both spacings. Do not alter the spacing if the studs do not come out even; instead, simply set the last two studs closer together. Mark the top plate also for the framing of a door, if you plan to have one in the wall (pages 34-35). Finally, set the top plate alongside the sole plate and transfer the markings to the second plate; use a carpenter's combination square to be sure that the new markings line up with the old.

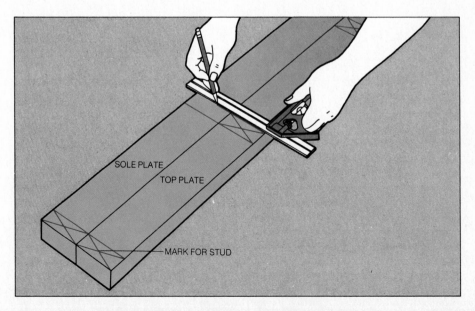

SOLE PLATE

TOP PLATE

MARK FOR STUD

2 **Assembling the frame.** To determine the length of the studs, measure along a plumb line dropped from the ceiling to the floor at each end of the new wall and at one point in the middle—the three measurements should agree within a fraction of an inch. Cut 2-by-4 studs 3 inches shorter than this measurement to allow for the combined thicknesses of the top and sole plates. Set the top plate on its side on the floor, and nail the studs into place at the marked positions, with two 16-penny nails driven down through the top of the plate into each stud.

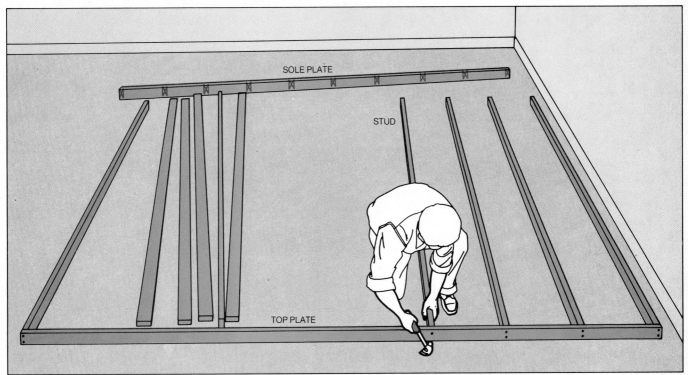

SOLE PLATE

STUD

TOP PLATE

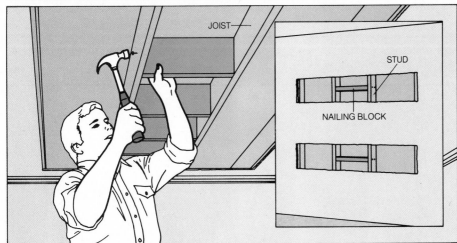

JOIST

STUD

NAILING BLOCK

3 **Finding or making frame supports.** If the new wall is to run across a number of joists, locate each joist (*page 10, Step 1*) and mark the ceiling at the joist positions. If the wall is to run parallel to the joists try to position it directly under one joist. If the wall must run between two joists, install nailing blocks no more than 24 inches apart to support the frame. Cut the blocks from lumber the same size as the joists, set the bottoms of the blocks flush to the bottoms of the joists and fasten each block with four 16-penny nails. If the space above the new wall is an unfloored attic install the blocks from above; if not, cut out a strip of ceiling board wide enough to expose about half the edges of the flanking joists (the total width is usually 48 inches). After installing the blocks patch the strip with new wallboard.

If the new wall meets an existing one between two studs (*inset*), install 2-by-4 nailing blocks at about one third and two thirds of the distance from floor to ceiling. Cut two holes in the wallboard to make the installation.

4 **Preparing the existing wall.** The new wall will probably meet an existing wall that is fitted with a baseboard at the floor and a molding at the ceiling; for a tight fit, you must remove the baseboard, the base shoe (a narrow strip sometimes fastened at the bottom of the baseboard) and the molding. Beginning at a corner or at the end of a strip, loosen the board, shoe or molding as much as you can without damaging it and insert a wooden wedge between it and the wall. Repeat the process, inserting wedges as you go, until the strip is completely detached.

5 **Installing the sole plate.** Drop a plumb line from the ceiling to the floor at several points along the line you have chosen for the top plate and have a helper mark the floor at these points; align the sole plate over the marks, butting it firmly against any existing wall that the new wall will meet. Fasten the sole plate to the floor with tenpenny nails at about 1-foot intervals.

SOLE PLATE

6 **Hanging the frame.** With the aid of a helper, lift the assembled wall frame onto the sole plate and hold it against the ceiling and the existing wall in the position you have chosen for it. While your helper holds the frame in place, fasten the ends of the top plate to the joists or nailing blocks overhead with 16-penny nails. Nail the outermost studs of the new wall to studs or nailing blocks in the existing one. Then nail the rest of the top plate to the joists or ceiling blocks.

TOP PLATE

7 **Toenailing the studs.** Set the bottoms of the studs directly over the sole-plate marks; use a carpenter's level to be sure the studs are absolutely vertical. Toenail the studs to the sole plate, using three tenpenny nails per stud—two on one side and the third centered on the other, so that the nails do not meet.

SOLE PLATE

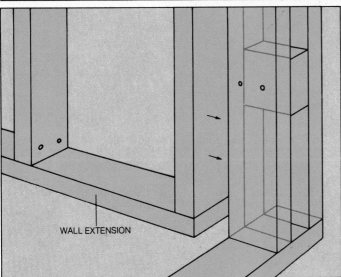

WALL EXTENSION

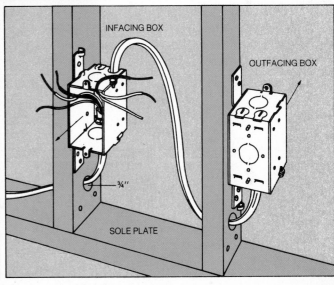

INFACING BOX

OUTFACING BOX

¾"

SOLE PLATE

8 **Turning a corner.** In a wall that turns at a right angle, reinforce the corner to make a firm attachment for the wall extension and its covering wallboard. Two inches back from the stud at the corner, install an additional stud; this stud can be put in when the frame is assembled on the floor or toenailed in place after the assembly is hung. Using tenpenny nails driven through the studs, fasten two 2-by-4 nailing blocks, each cut to a length of 2 inches, between the studs at points one third and two thirds of the distance from the floor to the ceiling. Use the blocks like nailing blocks in an existing wall (*page 29, Step 3*) to secure the wall extension.

9 **Roughing in wiring.** Before covering the frame with wallboard, decide upon the switches and outlets you want in the new wall, and mark positions for them on the nearest studs. Choose a route for wiring along the sole plate and drill ¾-inch holes through the studs along the route for running cable. Mount outlet boxes directly on the studs—use the flange-mounted type that is simply nailed to an exposed stud—and install cable in each box before the wallboard goes on; do not, at this point, connect the other end of the cable at the house circuit.

If you install outlet boxes that face in opposite directions, do not place them back to back: the two boxes will form a conduit for noise from one room to the next. Instead, install the boxes with at least one stud between them.

Knee Walls and Collar Beams

The sloping roof of an attic creates special problems in building walls—problems that call for ingenious adaptations of conventional techniques. At ceiling height, usually 7 feet 6 inches, collar beams convert two sloping surfaces to a single horizontal one, thick enough to attach the top plate of a conventional wall assembly (pages 30-31). At the ends of the beam, rafters are thickened by additional members called registers to provide nailing surfaces for cripple studs. And farther down the rafters, knee walls, usually 4 or 5 feet tall, convert a sloping surface to a vertical one. If your home was built before 1970, your rafters may be thicker than present-day lumber. In that case, use pieces of scrap lumber to thicken the nominal 2-by-4 blocking pieces between the collar beams. At the knee walls simply center the studs when you toenail them into the rafter.

1 Installing collar beams. At the location of the new wall, measure the ceiling height—usually 7 feet, 6 inches—from the floor to a rafter and drive a nail partway into the side of the rafter. Repeat on the opposite rafter, then measure the distance across the attic, through the nails to the sheathing of the roof. Cut two 2-by-6 beams ½ inch shorter than this distance, then cut the ends of the beams to conform to the roof slope (pages 68-69). Using three tenpenny nails at each end of the beams, nail a beam to each side of the selected rafter, with the bottoms flush to the ceiling mark and ¼-inch spaces between the beam ends and the roof sheathing. If the collar-beam span is 8 feet or more, nail short blocks of 2-by-4 between the beams at 3- to 4-foot intervals to keep the beams from bowing.

7' 6"

2 Building knee walls. At the sides of the attic, measure the height of the knee walls from the floor to the rafters and mark the rafters at that height. From the collar-beam rafter measure off the length of the new wall and cut two 2-by-4s to that length for the sole plates.

To build each knee wall, slide the sole plate into position, rest a vertical length of 2-by-4 on it, and trace the angle of the rafter on the 2-by-4. Cut the 2-by-4 to this mark and repeat the process at each rafter along the wall. Using a plumb line, mark the sole plate for the positions of the studs. Turn the sole plate on its side and attach each stud with two tenpenny nails driven through the sole plate and into the studs.

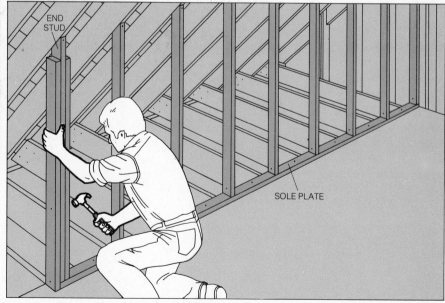

END STUD

SOLE PLATE

3 Installing the knee wall. Fasten the wall assembly in place. Use two tenpenny nails to attach the top of each stud to the underside of a rafter; use tenpenny nails at 1-foot intervals to anchor the plate to the floor, and 16-penny nails over joists. The end stud must be thickened to make nailing surfaces for wallboard. At the back of this stud, measure the distances from the rafter to the floor on one side, and from the rafter to the sole plate on the other. Cut two 2-by-4s to these lengths and nail them to the sides of the end stud with eightpenny nails.

4 **Assembling the center wall.** Measure the distance across the attic from one knee wall to the other and cut a 2-by-4 to this length to serve as the sole plate for the center wall. Attach the sole plate to the floor with tenpenny nails at 1-foot intervals, with the end of the plate meeting the inside end of the thickened knee-wall stud. Measure the bottom of the collar beams from rafter to rafter and cut a 2-by-4 to this length for a top plate. Complete this part of the wall exactly as you would a conventional partition (*pages 28-31*), by nailing studs to the top plate, nailing the top plate to the collar beam and toenailing the studs to the sole plate.

5 **Thickening the sloping rafter.** Measure along the rafter from the outermost center-wall stud to the end stud of the knee wall, and cut two 2-by-2s or 2-by-4s to that measurement to serve as registers. Nail the registers to opposite sides of the rafter, with the bottoms flush with the bottom of the rafter, using eightpenny nails. Cut a 2-by-4 to run from the center wall to the knee wall as a top plate, angling the ends to fit tightly against the stud at each end. Nail the top plate against the rafter and registers.

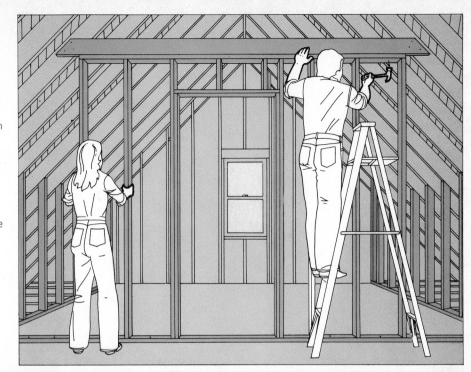

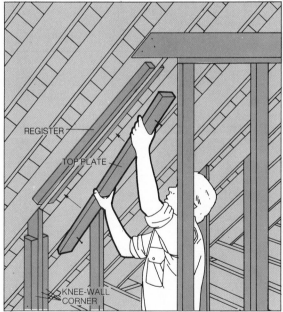

6 **Completing the center wall.** Mark the center-wall sole plate for a stud next to the knee-wall corner and for additional studs at 16- or 24-inch intervals from that point to the end of the center wall. Set lengths of 2-by-4 vertically on 2-by-4 scraps next to the marks, trace the height and angle of the rafter at the upper ends, and cut the 2-by-4s at the trace marks for studs. Toenail the studs into place between the top and sole plates with tenpenny nails; for a tight joint, fasten the first stud to the knee-wall corner with four eightpenny nails.

Making a Place for a Door

For an opening in a new partition—used as an open passageway between two rooms or closed off with a door—one or more regular wall studs must be eliminated. In their place is built a rigid supporting structure called a rough doorframe.

For a door, the rough frame must be built to an exact width and height based on the dimensions of the door unit. Buy the unit itself *(page 42)* from a lumber dealer before framing the opening, so you can make precise calculations beforehand *(below)*. If you plan to finish the rough opening with wallboard as an open passageway *(page 41)*, you can dispense with these calculations; simply space the outer studs 4 inches wider than the finished opening and cut the jack studs *(Step 1)* 1 inch shorter than the height of the opening.

A rough frame for a door. A doorway is framed into a new partition between two outer studs. Inside the outer studs a pair of jack studs supports a crosspiece called a header that forms the top of the frame. Short studs called cripples rise from the header to the top plate to brace the top of the frame and provide nailing surfaces for wallboard above the door.

Start the rough doorframe by installing two ordinary wall studs as the outer studs, according to the procedure on page 29, Step 2. These studs must be far enough apart to allow for all of the components shown at right that will eventually be installed in the opening: the width of the door; ⅛-inch clearances between the sides of the door and the jamb (or finish frame) in which the door will hang; the thickness of each side of the jamb (usually ¾ inch); clearances (usually ¼ inch each) between the side jambs and the jack studs; and the thicknesses (1½ inches each) of the jack studs. You will have to check the dimensions of the door and jamb to work out the correct positions for the outer studs.

The jack studs should be cut 1¼ inches shorter than the height of the jamb, thus allowing ¼ inch for clearance above the jamb, but subtracting 1½ inches for the thickness of the sole plate below the jack studs.

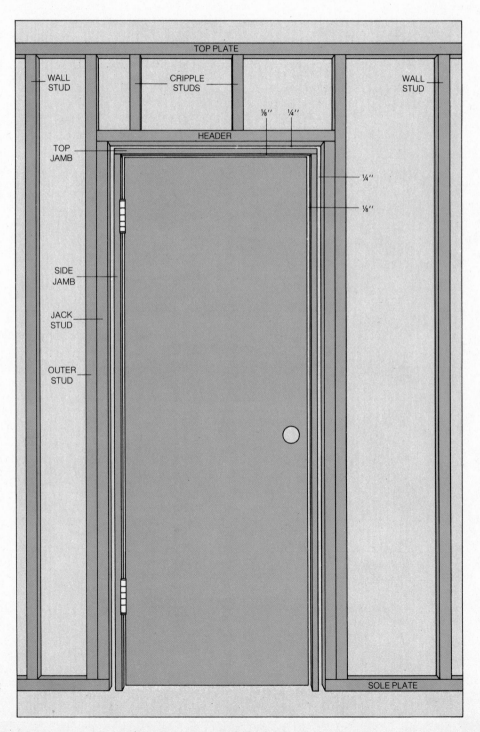

1 **Installing the jack studs.** Lay a jack stud against the inside of an outer stud with its bottom end even with the bottom of the outer stud. Bracing the outer stud with your foot, lean over and nail the jack stud to it with six 16-penny nails.

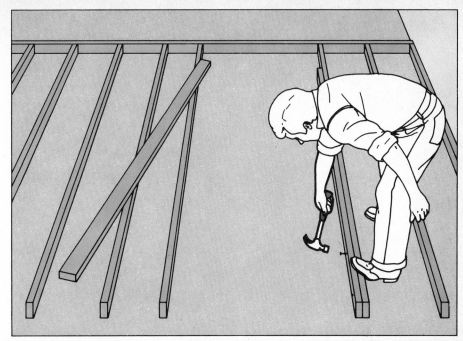

2 **Installing the header.** Cut a 2-by-4 to fit between the outer studs. Rest it across the tops of the jack studs and nail it into place with two 16-penny nails driven through each outer stud.

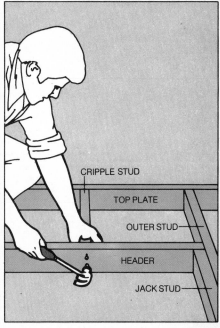

CRIPPLE STUD

TOP PLATE

OUTER STUD

HEADER

JACK STUD

3 **Installing the cripples.** Cut cripple studs long enough to extend from the top of the header to the top plate. These studs should be set at 16- or 24-inch intervals, like main wall studs at points where main studs would have been located within the doorframe. Fasten the cripple studs in place with 16-penny nails driven through the top plate and the header.

To complete the rough doorframe after raising the wall into position (*page 30, Step 6*), cut away the section of the sole plate from between the insides of the jack studs.

The Professional's Way with Wallboard

Wallboard, which is also called plasterboard, gypsum board, dry wall or Sheetrock, a trade name, is the common-sense solution for sheathing interior walls, much less costly and easier to install than wet plaster troweled over wood or metal lath. It is made of plaster, pressed into a sandwich, usually ½ inch thick, 4 feet wide and 8 feet long, with heavy white, gray or creamy paper on the front, and heavy kraft paper on the back.

The resulting sheet is not notably strong: it breaks if you bend it enough, and its corners crumble if you tip its 64-pound weight onto one of them. A stout hammer blow will punch right through it. But you can nail through it cleanly, break it neatly and quickly along a scored line, and saw it rapidly with any kind of wood saw. It will hold a hook strongly enough to hang light pictures, and it readily takes anchors of various types. If you have to cut into wallboard, you can patch it to its original smoothness, and it makes a good match for existing smooth plaster.

Making smooth joints to hide the seams between sheets takes practice. Using wallboard that has a slight bevel along the long edges makes the job easier. Adjacent bevels are filled in with joint compound—a homogenized, water-based plaster-of-paris filler-glue—reinforced by paper cover tape 2 inches wide. Outside corners are strengthened with angled metal strips called corner bead.

The joint compound is spread and feathered out with joint knives made especially for the task. Professionals use four widths—a 6-inch knife for applying the compound and embedding the tape, 10-inch and 12-inch knives for feathering out the next two applications and a 16-inch knife for extra feathering on butt joints that are not tapered. However, two joint knives—6 and 10 inches—will serve if you take care to make the applications as smooth as possible.

Wallboard is put up on walls after the ceiling (also, these days, usually made of wallboard) is finished. The standard 8-foot length fits the height of a wall built of commonplace 93-inch studs, but can be shortened for walls less than 8 feet high. For higher walls, you can buy wallboard in 10-, 12-, 14- and 16-foot lengths or you can apply sheets horizontally. On most ceilings, wallboard can be put up simply as shown on pages 78-79. Installing wallboard on a sloping ceiling such as above a stairway or under a gabled attic roof, however, is best left to the professionals; it is extremely difficult to fit the joints together, and nearly impossible for the nonprofessional to fill them smoothly with joint compound and paper.

If the board is to be nailed vertically, estimate your needs by measuring the perimeter of the room and dividing the number of feet by four. You will need an extra sheet or two for wastage. To install wallboard horizontally, treat each wall separately in making measurements.

Cutting the Sheets

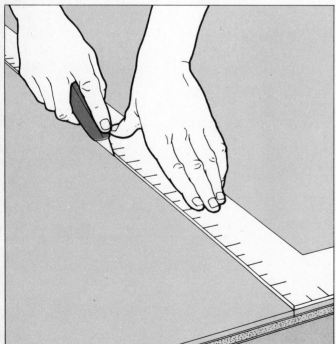

1 Scoring wallboard. Measure the size of the sheet needed and mark the face accordingly, using a carpenter's square and pressing hard with the pencil to indent the surface. Score the pencil line with a utility knife.

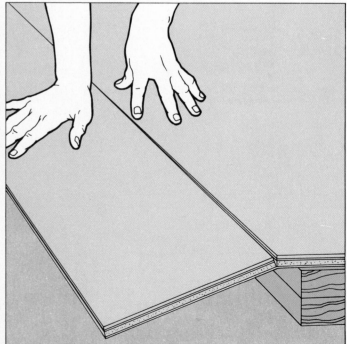

2 Snapping the core. Place two 2-by-4 scraps under the wallboard just behind the scored line. With the palm of your hand hit the outboard end of the sheet, snapping the core. Finish by slicing through the backing paper with a utility knife.

3 **Measuring for cutouts.** Cut holes for fixtures that will protrude through the wallboard before setting it in place. Measure the distance from the ceiling to the top and bottom of the fixture. Record the measurements on the face side of the board with pencil marks. Next measure the width of the cutout—the distance from the corner or the adjacent fastened sheet to both edges of the fixture—and make corresponding marks. Connect the marks to outline the hole.

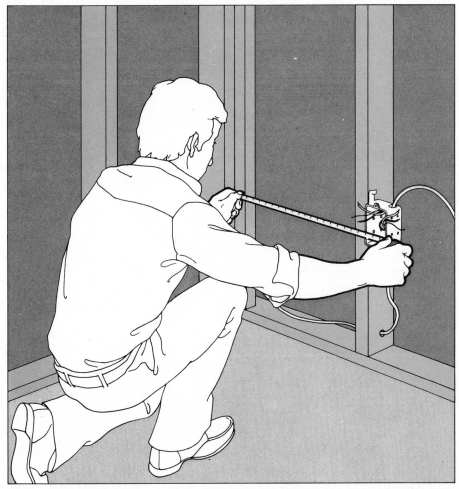

Eight Tips for a Smooth Job

☐ Stack and store wallboard flat on the floor; if it leans it may bow or break.

☐ Cut wallboard short instead of long to fit into a given space. The baseboard will cover up to 1½ inches of space at the bottom of the board. Trying to force wallboard into too small a space crumbles the edges.

☐ Be sure you get wallboard with beveled edges for ease in finishing the joints with joint paper and compound.

☐ Perforated tape, which has holes for joint compound to seep through, is easier to embed than plain tape.

☐ Premixed joint compound is easier to work with than the dry form. It always has the same consistency and will retain its moisture content for a year after being opened and resealed.

☐ Applying wallboard horizontally gives you the advantage of fewer joints to finish although the weight of longer lengths makes placing it a two-person job. It is the best method for high-ceilinged rooms and for hallways, where vertical joints are especially noticeable.

☐ Take safety precautions when you are working with dried joint compound, whether sanding new compound or removing old. Wear a face mask, goggles and hat to keep the dust out of lungs, eyes and hair.

☐ Don't rush the job. Ignoring wrinkled joint paper or uneven joint compound and taking nailing shortcuts might save installation time, but can result in split joints and popping nails.

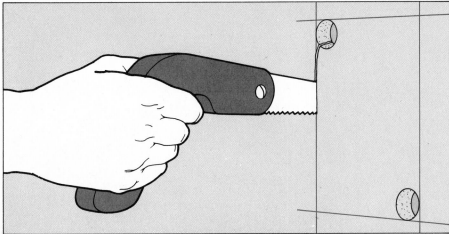

4 **Cutting for fixtures.** Drill holes in two diagonally opposite corners of the penciled shape. Force a keyhole saw through the board and cut along the lines. Raise the sheet into place and nail.

Installing the Sheets

1 Positioning the board. Mark the ceiling and floor to indicate the centers of the studs. Lean the first sheet into position in a corner. Shove a piece of wood shingle under the bottom, slide a scrap under the shingle, and use them as a foot-operated lever and fulcrum to push the sheet up against the ceiling and hold it there. Align the edge away from the corner with the center line of the stud. Using the ceiling marks to indicate the location of studs now behind the sheet, drive one annular wallboard nail into each stud about 1 foot down from ceiling. These fastenings will hold the board in place, and you can let up on the lever.

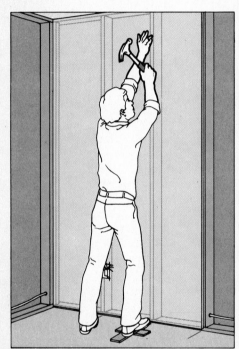

2 Nailing the board. Drive pairs of nails into each stud 2 inches apart at intervals of about a foot between pairs. At seams, nail ⅜ inch in from the edges. Between the edges, use the marks on the floor and ceiling to help nail into studs you cannot see. If you miss, pull the nail and try again; joint compound will later fill the hole. Drive each nail flush, then hammer again to set it a fraction of an inch below the surface *(inset, top)*. Be careful not to make this blow so hard you break the paper covering *(inset, middle)*, or hit it at an angle with the same result *(inset, bottom)*. Dimpling the nails allows the heads to be covered with joint compound and hidden.

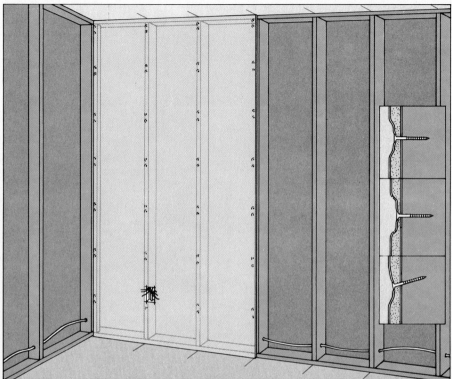

3 Fitting around windows and doors. For a window, measure down from the ceiling to the top and bottom of the jamb on both sides and across from the last installed sheet to the closest side jamb edge. (Trim will cover the spaces between the projecting ends of the jambs at the top and bottom of the window.) If the sheet will surround the window, also measure to the farthest side jamb edge. Mark these distances on the face of the sheet; connect the marks.

If the sheet will enclose three sides of the window, cut along the two parallel lines with a keyhole saw *(right)*. Then score the remaining line and snap the score *(page 36, Steps 1 and 2)*. If the sheet will surround the window, drill holes at the corners and cut with a keyhole saw.

For a door, mark only the distances from the ceiling to the jamb top and from the last installed sheet to the side jamb edge—or edges. Make all cuts with a keyhole saw.

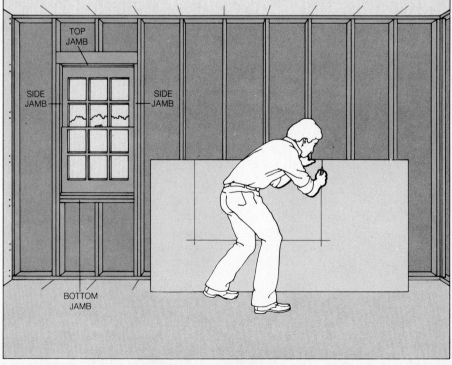

A Horizontal Pattern for Special Cases

Putting up the board. Mark the stud positions on the ceiling and floor. Drive eightpenny nails partway into the studs 4 feet down from the ceiling. With a helper, lift the wallboard so it butts against the ceiling, resting on the nails. Secure the wallboard by nailing it to the intermediate studs about a foot from the ceiling. Then finish nailing (*Step 2, opposite*) and remove the eightpenny nails. If the wall is more than 8 feet high, put up the second sheet similarly.

Before putting up the bottom sheet, measure from the bottom of the last installed sheet to the floor in at least four places; the ceiling and floor rarely will be parallel. Mark these distances on the new sheet. If the distances are fairly uniform, snap a chalk line between the marks, then score and break the sheet. Otherwise connect the marks with separate straight lines and cut the sheet with a keyhole saw. With a helper, raise the wallboard—using two fulcrums and levers—and nail in place.

Making Repairs with Wallboard

Replacing sections of wallboard. Cut new sheets to fit the opening and nail them after straightening the existing edges and cleaning off any bits of tape or joint compound. If you made the opening by cutting along stud edges, you must provide nailing surfaces for the wallboard; simply nail 1-by-2s inside the end studs so that they will be flush with the stud surfaces. For a small hole, extend the edges to the nearest studs and put up 1-by-2 nailing strips.

Replacing plaster with wallboard. Wearing a respirator, goggles and hat, extend the opening to the centers of the nearest studs with a chisel. Straighten the top and bottom edges with a keyhole saw. Remove the lath, using metal shears to cut the wire. To cut the surface of the wallboard patch flush with the plaster surface, nail strips of new lath across the studs at the top and bottom of the opening and at 16-inch intervals in between *(above)*, shimming them as

necessary. Mark the positions of the new nailing surfaces on the plaster wall. Alternatively, if the studs are in line and no shimming is needed, nail a scrap of ¼-inch plywood, cut to the size of the hole, across the opening. Cut the wallboard to fit the hole and nail (*Step 2, opposite*).

Concealing the Joints

1 Applying joint compound to seams. Ladle premixed joint compound into a baking pan long enough to accommodate a 10-inch as well as a 6-inch joint knife. Using the 6-inch knife, spread compound like butter to fill the trough formed by the tapered edges of the wallboard, with a layer covering the adjacent surface approximately 1/16 inch deep. (To fill joints at corners, follow the instructions on the opposite page.) Run the knife down the joint in one motion to smooth out the compound. Wipe the knife frequently against the lip of the pan; otherwise the compound will harden on the knife and score grooves in the wet compound.

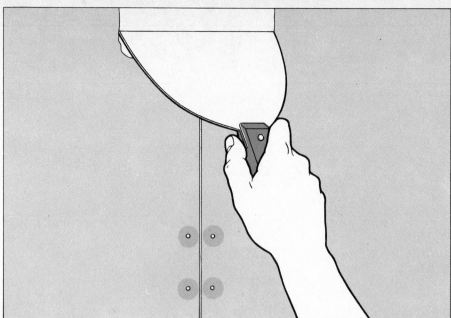

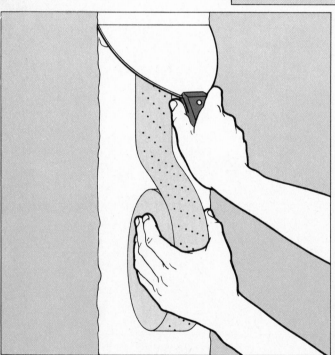

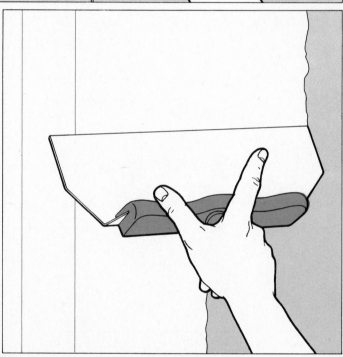

2 Taping the joint. With your finger, press one end of the perforated tape into the wet compound at the top of the joint. Unwind the tape with one hand and use the other hand to embed the tape in the joint compound with the knife. Watch for air pockets and wrinkles in the tape; if they appear, lift the tape, pull it tight, and embed it again. If the tape is badly wrinkled, peel it up and tear off the damaged section. Start again with fresh tape, positioning the ends of the sections as close together as possible. Tear the tape off the roll when you reach the bottom.

3 Feathering the joint. As the tape is embedded, compound will squeeze out along the sides of the joint. Run the knife down each side, spreading the compound outward. Press hardest on the outside edge of the knife so the compound gradually spreads to a feathered edge. Apply joint compound to the nail dimples on the intermediate studs, feathering the edges. A day later, apply a second coat to the joints with a 10-inch taping knife, feathering about 10 inches on either side of the joint. After another day, apply a third layer of joint compound, thinned with water until it is the consistency of pancake batter, and feathered just beyond the 10-inch line.

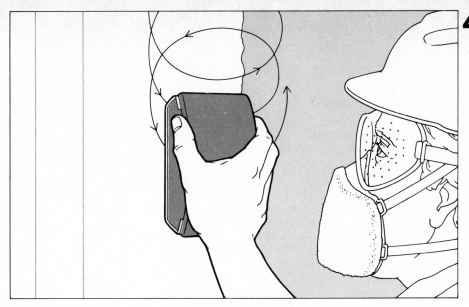

4 **Smoothing the surface.** When the last coat of compound is completely dry, smooth the surface with 100-grade garnet sandpaper on a sanding block, working in a circular motion from top to bottom. Similarly, sand over the filled-in nail dimples. Caution: Much dust is generated. Wear protective goggles, respirator and hat and keep the working area well ventilated.

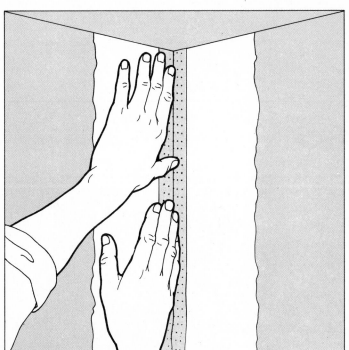

Taping inside corners. Use the 6-inch knife to slather joint compound into the crack in the inside corner of a wall or between a wall and the ceiling, buttering the compound in crosswise. Run the knife along each side of the joint to smooth the compound. Using one 2- to 3-foot-long strip at a time, bend the paper tape in half where it is creased for this purpose. Press the crease lightly into the corner by running your fingers along the joint. Draw the knife along each side of the joint, embedding the paper and feathering the edges. When applying the second and third coats do one side at a time. Allow the compound to dry one day between coats.

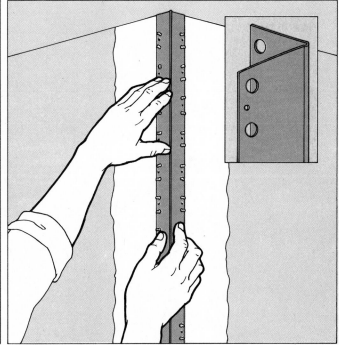

Strengthening outside corners. Butter a ⅛-inch-deep layer of compound over both sides of the corner. Press a reinforcing strip of metal corner bead (inset) into the compound so it fits flat on each side—you can nail it if you want to, but it should stick without nailing. Run the knife from ceiling to floor, smoothing out the compound that oozes through the perforations, and feathering. Apply two more coats of compound at one-day intervals. When completed, the rounded tip of the metal bead will still show but will be covered by the wall finish.

A Factory-fitted Door, Ready to Nail In

Time was when apprentice carpenters got out of bed slowly to face the task of finishing a doorframe and hanging the door. The craftsman had to erect a plumb and square doorjamb, the frame in which a door hangs; add a doorstop, the strip around the inside of the jamb that keeps the door from swinging too far through when closing; mortise recesses for the hinges; then fasten the door in place. Finally, he would attach the casing, the trim that frames the jamb and hides the ragged edges of plaster or wallboard around the door opening.

Fortunately, lumber mills have eliminated much of this travail by prehanging doors from accurately cut and smoothed jambs. Clearances are machine-checked, and before shipment the casing is permanently fixed to jambs that come apart for ease in installation.

Put up a prehung door after the wallboard has been installed (pages 36-41) but before the floor covering is laid (pages 64-67) and the room is trimmed (pages 46-49). To erect the door, pull two halves of the jamb apart, push one half into each side of the door opening, make adjustments and nail the assembly in place. The line where the two jamb halves meet is cleverly hidden under the doorstop.

Most lumberyards stock prehung versions of both louvered and flush doors, the two best-selling types. The standard height is 6 feet 8 inches and there are three standard widths: 24 inches for closets and small bathrooms; 32 inches for most other rooms; and 30 inches for small bedrooms or other locations where a 32-inch door would obstruct traffic when open. If you want a special size or style of door, your dealer can generally order it prehung from his supplier.

The jambs for prehung doors vary in thickness. A 4⅝-inch jamb is standard for use in framed walls covered with wallboard. Plaster walls are thicker and require a 5⅜-inch jamb.

After emplacing the door, you will install the lockset (page 44), which includes knobs, a latching mechanism and a strike plate that provides an aperture for the latch and prevents the latch from marring the jamb as the door closes. Despite the name, some locksets have no lock but only a latch. Others, appropriate for bathrooms or bedrooms, lock from the inside with a button—an emergency key can unlock them from the outside.

Prehung doors often come with holes predrilled to accommodate a standard lockset. If not, or if you have ordered an undrilled door in order to install an unusual lockset, use a hole saw—a rotating blade mounted in an electric drill—to cut a hole for the knobs. You will also bore a channel for the bolt and cut recesses for the bolt plate and the strike plate if these have not been precut.

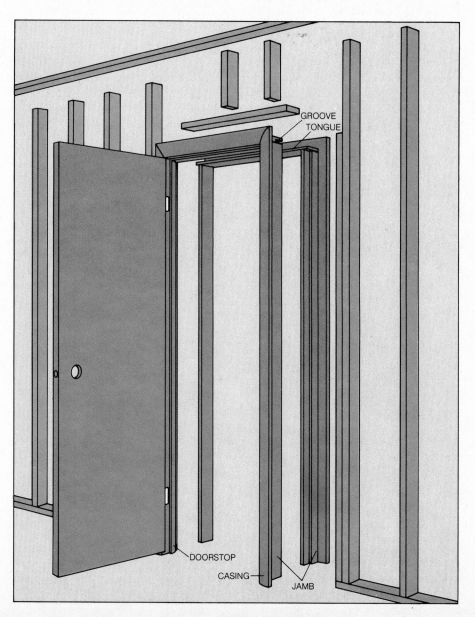

A prehung door. This factory-made unit consists of a door already hinged to the inside of a jamb, with the casing and doorstop attached. The jamb comes split so that each half can be pushed into the door opening with the casing still attached. The doorstop hides the tongue-and-groove joint that joins the two halves of the jamb.

To separate the jamb halves before starting work, first carefully remove the shipping braces. Next, pull the nail that holds the door closed. Leave in place any small cardboard strips wedged between the door and the jamb; they will serve as shims to maintain clearance between the door and the jamb while you work.

Installing the Jamb

1 Setting the door in place. Slide the half jamb attached to the door into the rough-framed wall opening (*pages 34-35*). Support the door on some scrap wood or a stack of magazines. Sight around the perimeter of the door and carefully adjust the position of the jamb—it has about ¼ inch of play—to leave about a ⅛-inch clearance between the door and the top and strike sides of the jamb. If the clearance at the top is uneven after the side jambs are adjusted, you may have to plane the bottom of one of the jamb legs.

If there are no previously inserted cardboard strips between door and jamb, shove scraps of shim—such as wood shingles—between the door and the jamb to hold the ⅛-inch clearance. Fasten the casing with eightpenny finishing nails driven into the wall every 12 inches or so.

2 Shimming the jamb. In a properly made rough frame for a door (*pages 34-35*) there will be a space of ¼ to ½ inch between the frame and the jamb. To keep the jamb from bowing outward over the years, insert two shims over the top of the jamb and three along each side; on the hinge side, two of the three should be placed just below the hinges and the third in the center. The shims should not extend beyond the jamb edges; score them at the jamb's edge and break off the protruding ends by smacking them with a hammer. At each shim, drive two 16-penny finishing nails through the jamb and the shims and into the rough frame.

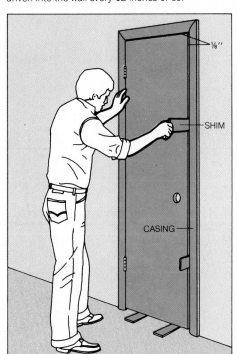

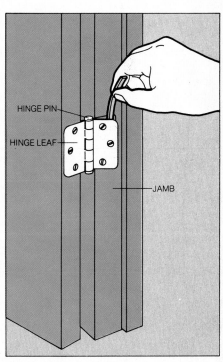

3 Completing the jamb. Slide the other half of the doorjamb into position, taking care to engage its tongue in the groove of the jamb half already in place. Press the casing snugly against the wall and nail it in place with eightpenny finishing nails driven through the casing and into the framing every 12 inches. Drive 16-penny finishing nails through the jamb and into the rough framing at similar intervals. Remove the shims wedging the door closed and check for smooth operation. Set all nails with a nail set and cover them with wood putty.

4 Making final adjustments. If a door binds or is too far from the strike side of the jamb, you can make small adjustments without removing it. Loosen the screws that anchor the hinge leaf to the jamb and insert a narrow strip of cardboard—or plastic cut from a bottle—behind the hinge leaf. Position this shim along the edge near the hinge pin to move the door away from the hinge side of the jamb and toward the strike side; position it along the edge farthest from the pin to move the door in the opposite direction. Retighten the hinge-leaf screws.

Caution: because any shift in the position of one side of the door moves the other three sides, the elimination of a bind at one point may create a bind at another. If you cannot straighten the door by shimming, remove it and plane the edges.

Installing the Lock

1 Marking for the knob. Because one edge of a door is beveled slightly to keep its corner from hitting the jamb as the door is closed, all measuring for lock and knob placement must be done on the so-called high side of the door—the face away from the doorstop. Working about 36 inches off the floor (or, still better, matching the height of other doorknobs in the house), measure in from the edge to locate the center of the knob; the proper distance is in the directions provided with your lock, technically called a lockset, and there may also be a cardboard template for more accurate positioning.

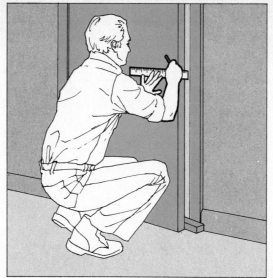

2 Marking for the bolt. On the edge of the door and at exactly the same level as the center of the doorknob hole, measure in from the high side to locate the center of the channel for the bolt. This distance, too, is specified in the directions.

3 Cutting for knobs and bolt. Use a hole saw of a diameter specified by the lockset instructions to cut a hole through the door for the knobs. To prevent splintering, cut from one side of the door until the drill bit at the center of the saw just breaks through the other side. Withdraw the saw and finish cutting from the other side, starting the saw in the proper position by inserting the center bit into the small hole.

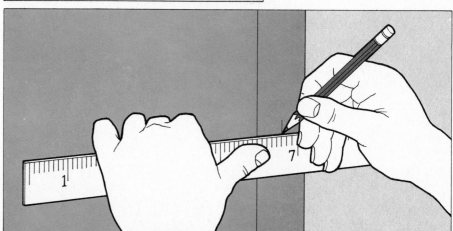

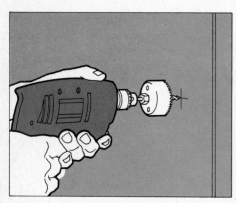

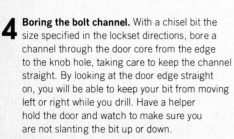

4 Boring the bolt channel. With a chisel bit the size specified in the lockset directions, bore a channel through the door core from the edge to the knob hole, taking care to keep the channel straight. By looking at the door edge straight on, you will be able to keep your bit from moving left or right while you drill. Have a helper hold the door and watch to make sure you are not slanting the bit up or down.

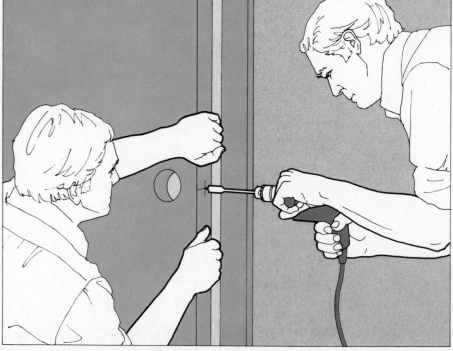

5 **Locating the strike.** Insert a short pencil through the bolt channel by way of the knob hole. Holding the door closed, run the pencil around the channel to trace a circle on the inside of the doorjamb for the location of the strike. With the same bit used to bore the channel, make a hole about ½ inch deep through the circle to provide a nest for the bolt.

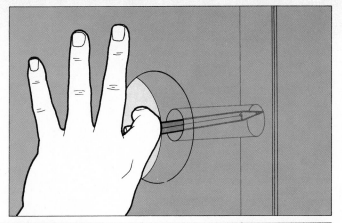

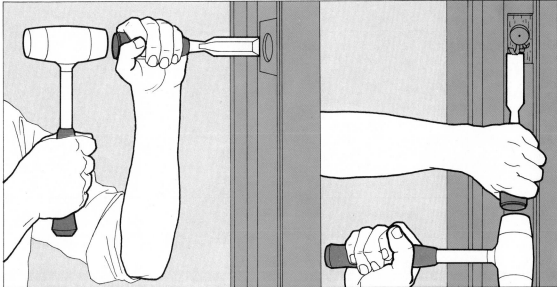

6 **Mortising the strike plate.** Hold the strike plate in place over the hole made in Step 5 and scratch around it with an awl or nail. To make the strike plate lie flush with the inside of the doorjamb, hold a chisel perpendicular to the doorjamb with its beveled side toward the mortise area and tap around the strike-plate outline to make a small cut approximately the depth of the plate (*above*). Then, holding the chisel at a low angle to the wood with its beveled side down, tap out a series of shallow cuts (*above right*); many short cuts make a smoother mortise than a few longer ones. Finish by using the chisel alone to shave the mortise to the exact depth needed. Screw the plate into the mortise.

Push the bolt assembly into the channel and scratch around it on the door edge with an awl. Remove the assembly and cut another mortise so the bolt plate is flush. Screw it into place.

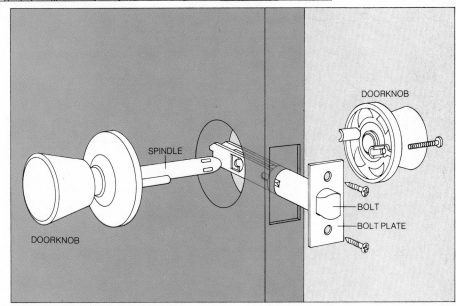

7 **Assembling the knobs.** Depress the bolt slightly and insert the doorknob spindle through the hole in the bolt assembly. Slip on the other doorknob and screw the assembly together.

Moldings for a Neat Finish

Floor moldings add finishing touches to a room and also cover up ragged wallboard ends and gaps between the flooring and the wall. In many rooms, particularly those with high ceilings, ceiling moldings fill a similar purpose at the corner between wall and ceiling.

Install moldings after you have finished work on the walls, ceiling and floor. Before painting the room, install the baseboard, which covers the joint between the wall and the flooring, and the ceiling molding. The base shoe, which seals the joint between the baseboard and the floor, is generally stained rather than painted and is therefore installed last.

Baseboard and ceiling moldings are generally stocked in pine but can be ordered—at considerable expense—in other woods. Base shoe is commonly stocked in both pine and oak (to match oak flooring). Moldings come in precut standard lengths of 6, 8, 10, 12, 14 and 16 feet. Measure each wall individually for both floor and ceiling. These measurements may differ, since walls are rarely straight from top to bottom. Buy appropriate lengths of molding for each wall to avoid either wasting material or having to piece out strips of molding by splicing.

When measuring, add 2 inches for each angle to be cut at the ends of a length of molding, remembering that at doorways floor molding is butted square against the door casing *(page 49)*. For a 12-foot-4-inch wall, for example, you will need 12 feet, 4 inches of molding and will therefore buy a 14-foot length. Measure and cut your base shoe after the baseboard has been installed, since the addition of the baseboard will alter the dimensions of the room.

The Fine Art of Mitering

Cutting baseboard and base shoe. To cut baseboard or base-shoe molding to fit an interior corner, mark straight across the top of the molding an inch or so in from the end. Without covering the mark, press a strip of masking tape down the face of the molding along the line of the cut to prevent splintering. Set the saw guide of a miter box at a 45° angle and position the molding in the box so that the wall side of the molding, when cut, will be longer than the front side. Cut the floor molding from left to right for the left-hand side of the corner and from right to left for the right-hand side.

To fit molding to an exterior corner, position the molding in the box so that the wall side of the molding, when cut, will be shorter than the front side. Measure and tape, then cut from right to left for the left-hand side of the corner and from left to right for the right-hand side.

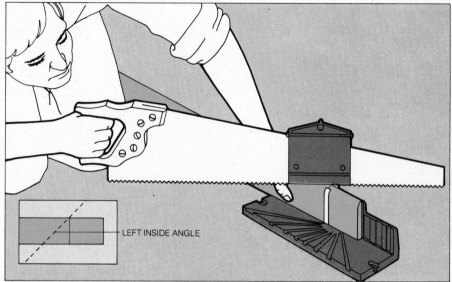

LEFT INSIDE ANGLE

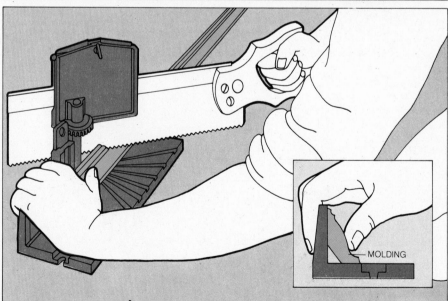

MOLDING

Cutting ceiling molding. To cut ceiling molding for a mitered corner, mark the guideline on the bottom edge of the molding. Place the molding in the miter box upside down, i.e., with the mark upward, and with the molding's two flat surfaces against the side and bottom of the box. As with floor moldings, cut so the wall side is longer than the face side for an interior corner and vice versa for an exterior corner. Since the molding is upside down in the box, cut from left to right for the left-hand side of an interior corner and from right to left for the right-hand side. Reverse this procedure for cutting the two sides of an exterior corner.

Cutting a miter-lap joint. Occasionally you may have to splice two lengths of floor or ceiling molding. Locate a stud near the point where you want to splice. Mark the top of the molding at the center of the stud and miter it at a 45° angle with the molding positioned so that the cut bisects the mark.

Similarly, miter another piece of molding at the same angle but in the opposite direction. With the molding in position against the wall, butt the angled cuts together. Drive a fourpenny nail through the spliced ends and into the center of the stud. Paint will hide the splice, but stain will not, so avoid splicing base shoe if possible.

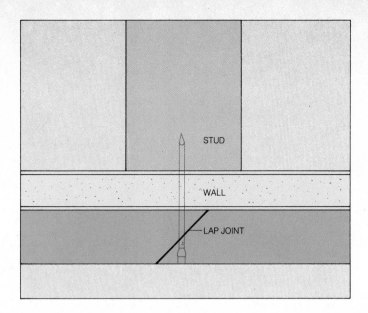

Making the Corners Fit Exactly

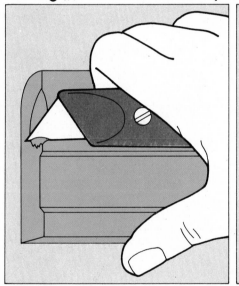

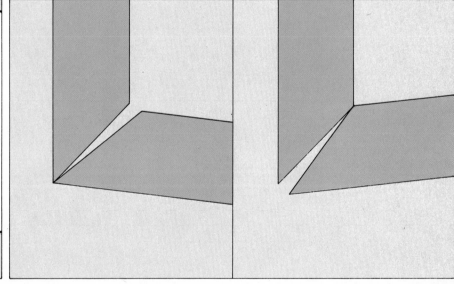

Feathering exterior angles. To ease the fit of molding at exterior corners, cut a crescent-shaped piece out of the angle-sawed end of the molding with a utility knife or coping saw. Begin the cut half an inch below the top of the molding; cutting out any portion of the top will create a visible gap in the joint. Cut inward and down to the bottom.

Making angles fit. Since corners in a room seldom make exact 90° angles, the angles of mitered molding joints must usually be widened or narrowed to fit corners perfectly before the molding is nailed in place. If the joint gaps on the wall side *(above)*, increase the angle formed by the two strips of molding by shaving away the fronts of the angled cuts with a utility knife, checking the fit frequently. If the joint gaps on the face side *(above, right)*, decrease the angle by shaving away the back portions of the cuts.

The mitering procedure is the same for both exterior and interior corners and for all types of both floor and ceiling molding. In every case, shave away the fronts of the mitered cuts to increase an angle and the backs of the cuts to decrease an angle. Make a double check of all the angles at each end of any strip of molding involved before nailing the molding in place.

The Right Way to Nail Molding

Fasten molding in place with the same care used in cutting or in correcting angles. The strips can pull away from the wall if they are incorrectly nailed, and a misplaced hammer blow can easily dent the soft pine generally used for molding.

After making sure that joints are properly fitted, begin nailing a strip of molding at one corner and continue across the room to the opposite end. If the wall is longer than your molding or if the length of a strip of molding proves unwieldy, cut and splice as described on page 47. Remove from the path of the molding any irregularities—such as accretions of paint on old walls or lumps of joint compound at the top or bottom of newly installed wallboard—that might keep the molding from fitting tightly.

Before finishing molding, set the nails about ⅛ inch into the wood and fill the holes with wood putty.

Fastening baseboard. Affix baseboard to the wall by driving two eightpenny finishing nails into the molding at each corner and at each stud. Drive one of the nails through the middle of the molding straight into the stud, and the other nail, at a 45° angle, into the sole plate near the bottom of the molding.

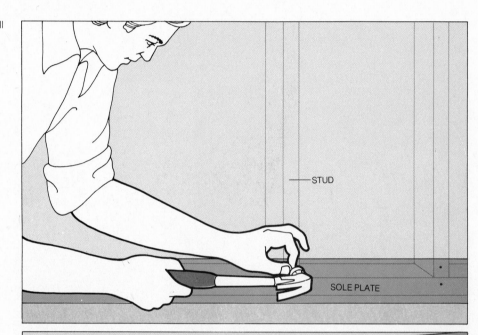

STUD

SOLE PLATE

Fastening ceiling molding. Attach ceiling molding by driving nails straight through the middle of the molding at corners and into the studs. Use eightpenny finishing nails—or longer nails if the molding is particularly heavy. Nailing up long strips of molding requires a helper to hold up one end. If you must work singlehanded, cut miter laps at 5-foot intervals, and fasten each strip by nailing it first to the stud nearest the middle of the strip, then nailing back toward one end of the strip and finally nailing forward to the other end.

STUD

Finishing mitered corners. Hold the mitered ends of two strips of molding firmly together by driving fourpenny finishing nails through the molding into the wall close to the corner. For baseboard and ceiling moldings, drive two nails at each side of the corner; for the base shoe, drive one nail into the baseboard at each side.

Fastening the base shoe. Nail the base shoe to the floor with fourpenny finishing nails at intervals of about 16 inches. Drive the nail at a 45° angle downward into the floor just above the middle of the base shoe; nailing too near the top of the shoe can split the wood.

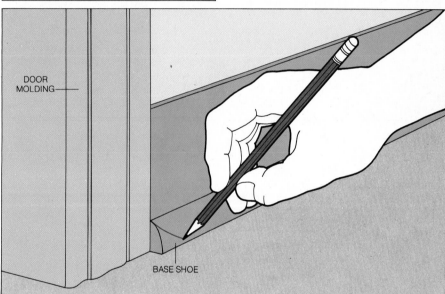

Fitting the base shoe to doorways. To improve the appearance of the base shoe where it juts into the room past the molding for doors, bookcases and other built-ins, sculpt the obtrusive end into a curve. Holding the base shoe in place, mark a freehand line on the base shoe. Begin the line at the point where the base shoe protrudes past the frame, and curve the line away from the frame. Set the base shoe on a solid surface, plane along the line and sand it smooth.

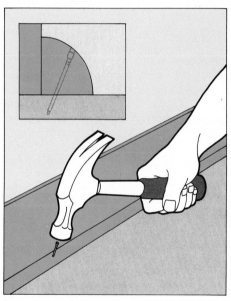

DOOR MOLDING

BASE SHOE

Marrying New Trim to Old

When you add a partition to a room, you may be able to buy new moldings that match. If so, set your miter box at a 45° angle and saw enough of the old molding for the run from its original corner to the new wall. Then miter the new molding and join it to the old.

If the molding is antique, and you cannot make a perfect match, the most practical, inexpensive and pleasing solution is not to make a match at all. Reproducing the pattern of antique molding is costly, and new molding that fails to match the old exactly is generally obtrusive. Use instead a plain new molding or clear pine board cut to the same height as the old molding. The new moldings in this application butt against the old walls. With the miter box set at a 90° angle, square-cut the ends of the new molding to fit their run, and nail them to the new wall. Using the same setting, cut the old moldings to lengths equal to the distance from their original corners to the face of the new moldings. Nail them into place.

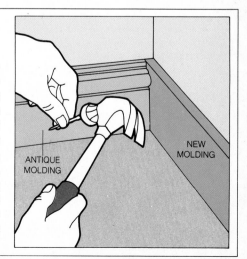

ANTIQUE MOLDING

NEW MOLDING

Removing Walls: Simpler Than You Think

Taking down a partition, even one structurally essential to the house, is a job well within the capability of most homeowners. Before you start, make sure you understand all of the wall's functions, and know how well they can be served when it is gone. Check to be certain that the space the wall divides will not seem ill-proportioned without it. Note that besides serving as a partition a wall may carry pipes, wires or heat ducts. Keep in mind that although removing a wall may join two spaces together it does not actually add any more space than the few square feet on which the wall stands.

To size up the job, look the wall over. The number of outlets and switches will suggest how much wiring lies inside it. A bathroom directly above may be hooked to plumbing that goes down through the wall. From the basement you may be able to detect whether heating pipes or conductors rise within the wall.

If all you find is wiring that terminates at outlets in the wall, you can remove it when you break the wall. A hot-air duct connected to a wall register can be cut back to the floor and capped with a grid. Even if you encounter many pipes and cables, you may be able to remove the bulk of the partition and leave part of one end of the wall to carry the various conductors, which can be moved there by a plumber or an electrician.

More critically, you should be aware that the wall may bear weight from above, thus serving as a vital structural element of the house. If it does, you will have to limit the width of the opening to 14 feet, because a bigger span entails too many risks and difficulties. To replace the weight-carrying function of the wall, you will have to install a visible overhead beam, as well as end posts for this beam that may also be visible, so that instead of removing the wall without a trace you make an arch. These intrusions can be minimized by surfacing the structural members with wallboard to match the walls, or by positioning furniture, such as bookcases, to hide the posts.

The key clue to a bearing wall is joists crossing its top plates perpendicular to them (diagram, right). You may be able to see the direction of the joists from your attic; you may have to cut a peep-hole in the ceiling next to the wall to be removed. The basement can also yield clues. If you find a girder or a wall running under and parallel to the partition in question, you can be quite sure that the partition carries weight down to this support. If any doubt remains, assume that the wall bears weight.

As the converse of a bearing wall, a nonbearing wall usually runs parallel to the joists and perpendicular to the long walls of the house. Walls enclosing small spaces like closets are probably nonbearing walls—but be sure to check. Because nonbearing walls serve no structural function, they can be removed without leaving an arch.

Tearing off the surfaces of the wall you are removing is not difficult, but prepare for dirty work, especially if the material is plaster. When the wall is gone, you will confront breaks in the ceiling, walls and floor. Ceilings and walls are easy to patch. The break in the floor of newly joined rooms can be built up with any wood as thick as the flooring, and the whole room carpeted or tiled. If the floors are of valuable hardwood and will remain exposed, you may need professional help to patch and refinish them.

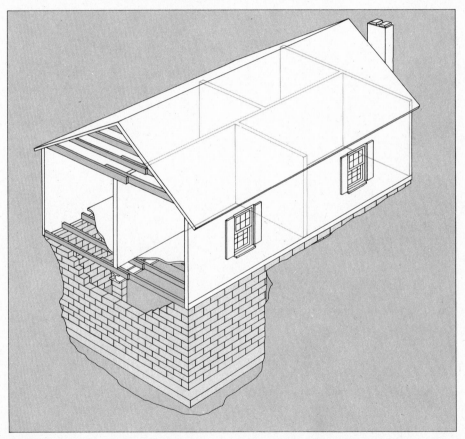

Bearing and nonbearing walls. This simplified diagram of a frame house shows how the cumulative weight of a house is passed down to its underground footings. Apart from the roof, which is supported by the outer walls parallel to the ridgepole, the weight load consists of the house structure itself plus whatever is on the floors, such as furniture, appliances, bathtubs or people. The joists under the floor are beams that transfer this load to the tops of the walls at both ends. The side walls that hold up one end of the joists carry the weight to the foundations, which take the burden to the footings. (End walls usually do not carry weight.) Since a single wood joist is neither long enough nor strong enough to span the usual distance from one side wall to another, house framers provide two joists and rest their inside ends on an interior bearing wall, such as the one that runs the length of the house shown in the diagram. The interior bearing wall carries the weight down to a solid support, sometimes a bearing wall that rests on its own footings, often to a steel girder whose ends rest on the foundation.

Taking Out a Nonbearing Wall

1 **Stripping the wall.** After you have determined that you can remove the partition without encountering any insuperable difficulties *(page 50)*, tear off the trim and turn off the electrical circuits to the outlets. Tape down dropcloths, wear a respirator and goggles, close doors and open windows. The wall surfaces can be cut out with a keyhole saw, but a hand circular saw, set to the thickness of the wall surface, will make a job of this size go much faster. Cut chunks of wall from between the studs, using a metal-cutting blade if the wall is plaster on metal lath. Saw the studs in two near the middle, and work the halves free from their nailing.

2 **Removing outlet wiring.** When you reach an outlet, remove its cover plate and strip off the wall surface around it. If the box is connected to a single cable coming up from a basement directly beneath, disconnect the cable from its receptacle and box, and tug at it while a helper in the basement watches to identify it by its movement. Trace the cable back to a junction box, disconnect it and pull it free from below. If the cable runs through studs toward an adjoining wall that contains a receptacle, this nearby outlet may be the source of power. Test first to see whether the current is off in both outlets. If it

is, clip a continuity tester to the black wire in the exposed receptacle box and with its probe touch the black wire in the neighboring outlet. A glow in the tester lamp proves that the cable runs between the outlets. Disconnect the cable from the box in the adjoining wall. Pull the dead cable out or cut it off short.

If you cannot trace a cable's origins, or if tearing off the wall reveals that the outlet is tied into the middle of the run of a cable, or if unrelated cables pass through the wall, you may need professional help to reroute the wiring.

3 **The last stud.** At the end of the partition, the last stud is nailed to a pair of close-set studs in the adjoining wall. In prying it loose, begin at the bottom and use a wide wood scrap held against the wall as a fulcrum for the pry bar so that the bar will not break through the covering of the adjoining wall. When the stud is safely away from the wall, wrench it free.

The top plate is usually nailed upward to blocks between adjacent joists. Pry it down, beginning at the nailhead nearest one end, using a wood scrap as a prying surface.

4 **The sole plate.** Somewhere near the center of the sole plate, make two saw cuts about 2 inches apart. Chisel out the wood between the cuts down to the subfloor. Insert a crowbar and pry up one end of the plate. With a scrap of 2-by-4 as a fulcrum, pry up the other end.

Repair the gaps made in the adjoining walls and the ceiling as described on page 39. If you are planning to cover the floor with resilient tiles or carpeting, fill in the space where the sole plate rested with a board thick enough to make the surface even.

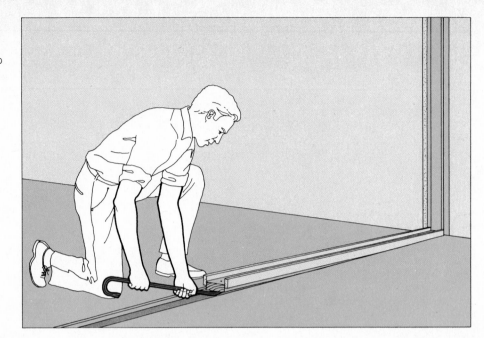

How to Leave a Section in Place

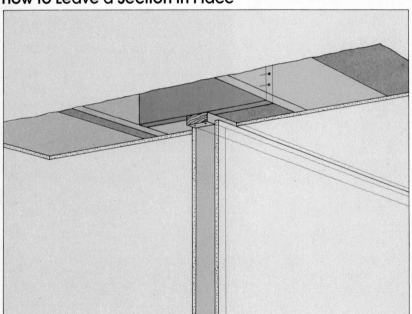

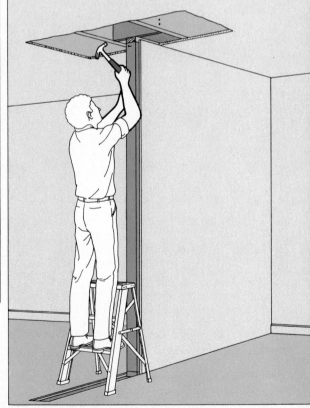

1 **Securing the top plate.** Remove the surface and studs (page 51, Steps 1-3)—but not the plates—of the wall back to the stud nearest the end of the part you wish to preserve. Cut a hole about 1 foot wide in the ceiling, centered on the upper end of the stud and running to the second joist on either side. Saw the upper plate off 1½ inches out from the stud, and pry down the part of it remaining over the opening. Butt-nail a block as wide as the joists between the joists on each side of the plate, resting the edge of the block on the outer end of the plate. Nail through the plate up into the block.

2 **Reinforcing the stud.** Saw the sole plate down to floor level 1½ inches out from the stud and chisel through the rest of it. Remove it as in Step 4, above. Nail a reinforcing stud, running from plate to plate, against the existing stud.

Surface the reinforcing stud with wallboard and finish it with tape and corner beads (pages 40-41).

Taking Out a Bearing Wall

The beam that will carry the weight hitherto supported by the wall is the main consideration when you plan to remove a bearing wall. For spans of up to 8 feet, make a wood header, choosing boards as directed in the table below. For wider spans use American standard 8-by-17 steel girders (i.e., 8 inches high and weighing 17 pounds per foot). Commonly called I beams, they are 5¼ inches wide and are sold by steel-supply dealers to the length ordered. Four-by-four posts are used to support the header beam.

Do not remove a bearing wall if the load above it is uncommonly heavy—a concrete-floored bathroom or a bedroom containing a water bed, for example. Even for ordinary weights, the posts that carry the load downward from the beam must rest on solid structure. For spans of up to 8 feet—a job most homeowners can confidently tackle—the posts can be positioned above joists in the floor, which carry the weight to the beam or other weight-bearing structure originally provided to support the wall.

In going beyond 8 feet with girders, the problems of post support become more critical, often demanding special blocking beneath the floor to bear the load downward. When you concentrate the weight once carried by the wall on two posts, you alter the structural design of the house; you may have to break into a lower ceiling, or consult an engineer, to determine whether all the supporting members below the post will be strong enough. Since the weight on the posts increases with the length of the span, amateurs should not attempt to bridge openings wider than 14 feet.

Wood headers that run to a side wall can rest on support posts within the wall, leaving an unbroken surface when the job is done. Allow 3½ inches of extra length on the end of a header that goes into a wall. The joists above a bearing wall need the support of temporary walls on both sides while the job is underway. If the temporary walls will block access to your working area, place the new header or girder next to the partition that must come down before you build the temporary walls.

1 **Building a wood header.** Cut a piece of ½-inch plywood the same size as the header pieces and sandwich it between them. Secure the sandwich by driving 16-penny nails through the boards from one side. If the header is to be fitted into an adjoining wall, cut a notch out of its upper corner 3 inches deep and 3½ inches long so it will fit around the top plate in the adjoining wall.

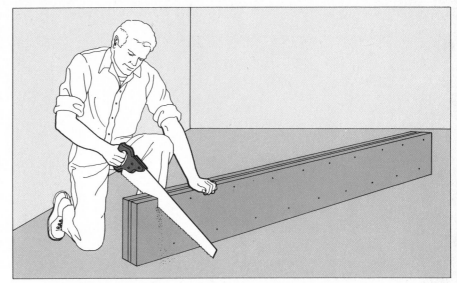

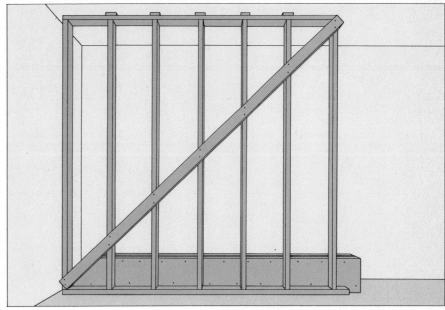

Header Dimensions

Maximum span	Board size
3'6''	2 × 6
5'	2 × 8
6'6''	2 × 10
8'	2 × 12

2 **Installing temporary support walls.** Using the procedure described on pages 28-31, put up stud walls about 30 inches out from the partition on both sides. In toenailing the studs, use double-headed nails for easy removal later. Brace the wall with a diagonal 1-by-4 nailed to every stud. The temporary wall should run the width of the span, but need not abut a side wall closer than 2 inches. Find the positions of the joists above (page 10), and shim tightly between them and the top plate, using pairs of shingles as wedges. Caution: make sure the support walls are vertical and firmly secured by their tight fit.

Remove the existing wall surface and studs in the manner shown on page 51, Steps 1-3.

3 **Prying out the plates.** The doubled top plates of a bearing wall are interlocked with those in the adjoining wall. To remove them, cut out a 2-inch chunk with a saber saw and begin prying a length of the doubled plate down far enough to use it as a lever. Get a firm hand hold on it and work it free from its nailing in the adjoining wall. Similarly remove the other section. Cut and remove the sole plate *(page 52, Step 4).*

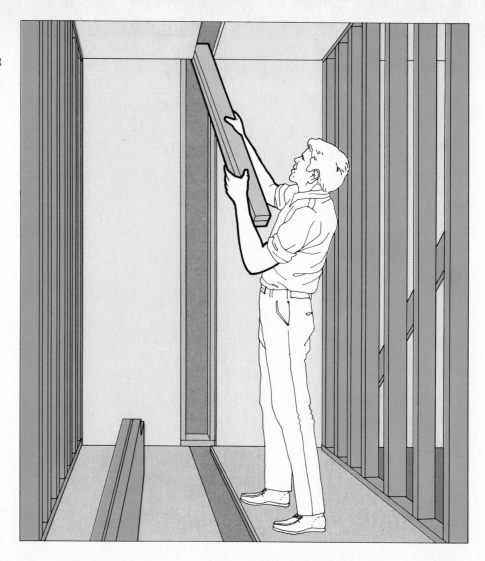

A Strong Base for Header Supports

The great weight that is held up by header supports must be transmitted directly downward through structural components to the foundation of the house. Usually header supports are placed on the sole plate of an adjoining nonbearing wall that runs perpendicular to the wall being removed. The plate transmits the weight to a joist directly beneath it, which in turn carries it to the top of a girder or bearing wall underneath *(top right);* the girder or bearing wall is supported by the house's foundation. But sometimes carpenters place the sole plate of a wall adjoining a bearing wall not above but between joists *(bottom right).* In this case the plate and post need special blocking under them to carry the weight directly downward to the

girder or bearing wall below. If you find there is no girder or wall directly below, consult an architect or contractor regarding proper placement of the posts.

To determine if blocking is needed, drive a nail through the subfloor next to the side-wall plate, find where it protrudes beneath, and determine whether the plate rests above a joist. If not, cut two pieces of board the width and thickness of the joists and long enough to run between the joists. Nail them together with six tenpenny nails and butt-nail them to the joists with two 16-penny nails for each board at each end. This blocking should fit snugly between the bottom of the subfloor and the top of the girder or wall below; any gaps above or below the blocking can be shimmed.

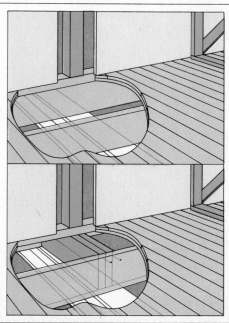

4 **Installing the header.** After the partition has been removed, the breaks in the side walls will reveal pairs of close-set studs placed to provide nailing for wall surfacing *(page 51, Step 3)*. Cut the wall back to the nearest studs on either side of these nailing studs, and pry the nailing studs free. Place the header, notched edge up, on the sole plates of the side walls for each end. Cut a 4-by-4 post precisely as long as the distance from the top of the resting header to the joist above it that runs nearest the wall. Check the posts to be sure they fit with no gap or surplus.

5 **Raising the header.** With helpers, raise the header to the joists. Check whether it fits flush against all joists; if the center ones are low, put the header down and raise the sagging joists by tightening the shims on top of the temporary walls. With the header in position, jam one 4-by-4 under each end. Use a level to get the post truly vertical. Toenail the post to the sole plate and the header. Nail a piece of 1-by-4 about 1 foot long to join the side of the header to the top of the 4-by-4 and to provide a nailing surface for the wallboard.

Remove the temporary walls. Patch the wall *(page 39)*. Surface the header with wallboard and corner beads *(pages 36-41)*.

Butting a Header to a Wall

1 Positioning support studs. Do not notch the header. Dismantle the wall surface and studs back to the stud nearest the desired end of the wing wall. Cut the doubled top plate flush with the stud and remove it (*page 54, Step 3*). Cut the sole plate 3½ inches out from the stud and remove the remainder (*page 52, Step 4*). Use the procedure described in the box on page 54 to ascertain whether the existing stud stands over a joist, and install blocking if needed.

2 Raising the header. Rest the header end on the protruding sole plate and cut two 4-by-4s exactly long enough to reach from the top of the header to the joist above nearest the stud. Raise the header and force one post between it and the sole plate. Drill through the post and stud and use four toggle bolts to secure the post, making sure to countersink their heads. Similarly, secure the second post. Cover the posts and header with wallboard and corner beads.

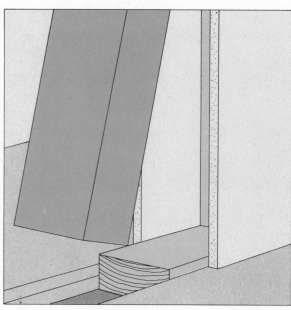

Bridging with Steel

1 Getting the girder ready. Purchase a girder 6 inches longer than the distance to be spanned. To make a place to store it temporarily, take off the wallboard in the side walls adjacent to the ends of the partition being removed, cutting back to the nearest stud. With assistants to help you swing and angle the girder, place it next to the wall with its ends resting on the sole plates in the side-wall openings. Remove the partition surface, studs and sole plate of the wall, following Steps 1-4 on pages 51-52, but do not remove the top plates. Cut 4-by-4 posts to fit exactly between the top of the resting girder and the bottom of the top plate. Check these posts to make sure that they fit snugly.

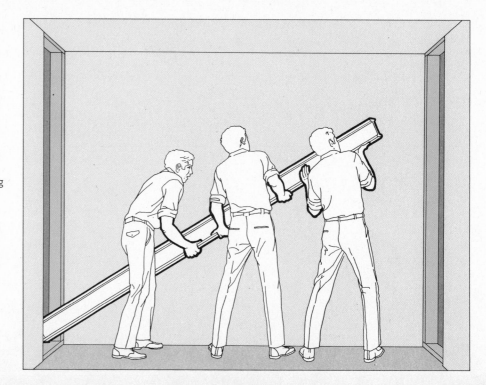

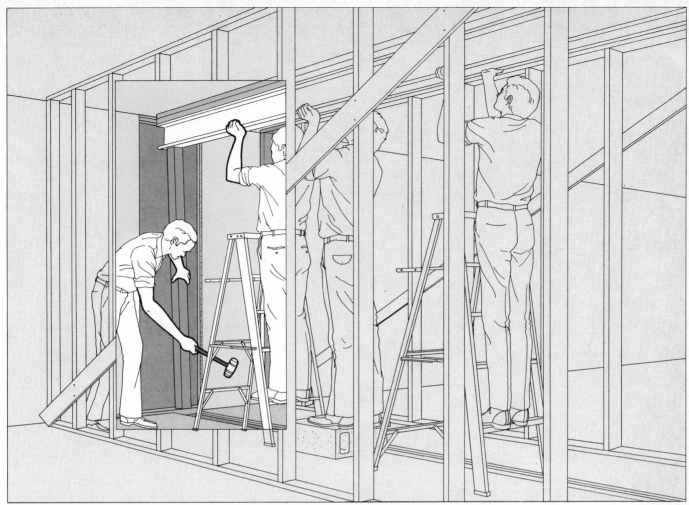

2 **Raising the girder.** Recruit one helper for each 3 feet of girder. If the ceiling is high, provide platforms, made of 8-inch concrete blocks set side by side, for them to stand on. Have the crew lift one end of the girder high enough to slide a stepladder under it about 2 feet from the side wall. Repeat, with another stepladder, at the other end. Raise the girder so that it is centered beneath the top plates. If the contact between the girder and the plates shows that the ceiling is sagging, put the girder back on the ladders and force the ceiling up by tightening the shims on the temporary walls. Tap the posts into position under the girder ends *(above)*, setting them so that they are exactly vertical.

3 **Securing and finishing.** Cut boards to fill the gap between the ceiling and the top flange of the girder. Nail them to the sides of the top plates. Cut a number of 1-by-2s that are ¾ inch longer than the distance from the ceiling to the bottom of the girder. Nail them 16 inches apart to the filler blocks and to the edges of a 1-by-6 held against the bottom of the girder.

Remove the temporary walls. Apply wallboard over the wood pieces covering the girder.

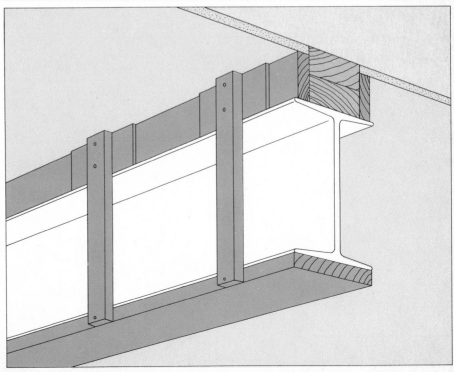

Solid Floors and Versatile Ceilings

3

Stapling up a ceiling. A staple gun makes quick work of attaching foot-square acoustic tiles to wooden furring strips nailed across ceiling joists. The sound-absorbing tiles, a popular choice for ceilings when rooms are rebuilt, are held in place not only by the grip of the staples but also by interlocking tongues and grooves.

Creating any new living space usually involves installing or replacing a floor or a ceiling or both. Just patching the existing surface is usually less satisfactory in the long run than putting in a new one. For one thing, you will want the kind of overhead shelter and underfoot support that both suit your taste and match the uses you plan for your new room. And in most cases putting in a new floor or ceiling requires very little more work than extensively repairing an old one.

Ceilings and floors constructed with forethought and a moderate outlay of time and money can contribute much to comfort and appearance. In many cases they make up for architectural deficiencies. Dividing a room, for example, may make the ceiling too high for the room size; lowering the ceiling restores proper proportions. Recessing light fixtures can make a low ceiling seem higher. Soundproofing a ceiling or a floor can deaden the upstairs or downstairs din and adapt a room for use as a study or a home office. By merely coloring or texturizing a floor you can change the whole look and function of a room: a basement becomes a children's playroom with tough, bright-bordered tiles underfoot; an enclosed garage turns into a study with silent, deep-toned parquet under a small area rug; an attic is transformed into a bedroom where cool-colored tiles catch and amplify the light from dormer windows.

Planning and preparation, essential to any home improvement project, are especially important in the case of floors and ceilings. Floors particularly demand solid foundations since they take more of a beating than any other surface in the house. A well-built floor like the one on pages 60-67 is much more than a surface; it is a many-layered structure starting, perhaps, from a slab that must be leveled and waterproofed, and continuing with joists or sleepers, subflooring, underlayment and finally a finish that can be anything from elegant parquet to colorful plastic.

Support for a ceiling is less complicated. Most ceilings are simply attached directly to the joists that support the floor of the room above or to furring strips nailed at intervals across the joists. Where no ceiling joists exist, as in an attic, you can nail collar beams across rafters *(pages 68-69)* and attach the ceiling to them. Hanging a suspended ceiling *(pages 70-71)* requires little more technical skill than hanging a picture; prefabricated snap-together metal strips strung from the joists provide a framework for drop-in panels.

Devising a pattern of tiles or panels to cover a floor or a ceiling tidily and symmetrically can be a fascinating exercise in practical geometry. By following the instructions on page 66 you can even fit floor tiles around corners and such irregularities as thresholds and doorjambs with professional ease.

Layered Flooring: Level, Smooth, Squeak-free

If a new floor is needed in the extra living space you set up, cemented-down tiles—made of any of a variety of materials *(pages 64-67)*—are the simplest to use.

Since they show every lump, bump and nailhead beneath them, or buckle unless seated properly, they must be laid over a perfectly smooth surface. The concrete slab of a basement or garage will serve if it is first leveled and waterproofed *(below and top right)*. Wood subfloors and existing finish flooring need to be covered with an underlayment of smooth ¼-inch hardboard or ⅝-inch plywood that is nailed in place as a base for the tiles.

In an attic both subflooring and under-layment may have to be added to existing joists, creating a complete floor like the one below, left. Subflooring must be laid before walls are built, underlayment afterward. If the joists are spaced more than 16 inches apart or made of lumber smaller than 2-by-8, you will need to increase or reinforce them *(opposite, center)*. The composite floor—joists plus subfloor plus underlayment—is also preferred on top of concrete, since the tiles are less likely to peel off, and the wood platform adds spring to make the result more comfortable to walk on than tiles that are in direct contact with concrete. To build this platform on a slab, you will have to add sleepers—joists placed on their sides.

Regardless of the type of floor installed over concrete, the slab itself should be moistureproofed first. A clear water-proofing solution, available at hardware stores and applied like paint with a roller or brush, will do the trick if your basement feels dry, and if you plan to tile or paint directly over it. For a raised floor, seal the slab with asphalt before putting down the sleepers *(opposite, top)*. Neither treatment, of course, will protect your flooring if you are plagued by water in your basement. This problem should be solved before any flooring is laid.

Anatomy of a floor. Whether upstairs or down, floors share a similar structure. At the bottom are the joists, called sleepers when atop a concrete slab, commonly spaced 16 inches apart. Resting on the joists is the subfloor, usually sheets of plywood ⅝ inch thick nailed to the joists.

An additional layer, called the underlayment, is recommended for the tile flooring shown here. Made of ¼-inch hardboard, it is nailed to the subfloor—but not the joists—to provide a smooth base. Topmost is the finish flooring of asphalt, vinyl or wood-block tiles, cemented in place.

Preparing a Concrete Slab

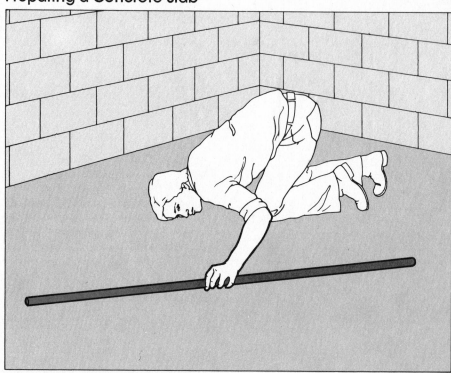

Leveling the slab. If tiles are to be cemented to concrete, check for irregularities by rolling a long straight piece of pipe over the surface while, from a low angle, you look for slits of light under the pipe. Flatten bumps of ¼ inch or more with a rub brick or a rented electric concrete grinder. Fill in low areas with a fast-drying cement-sand-epoxy compound—ask for flash patch, a filler compound that retains its resilience when set. Apply it with a trowel, then level the patches with a straightedge. When the patching compound dries—usually within 24 hours—waterproof the slab by applying clear waterproofing solution with a brush, roller or squeegee.

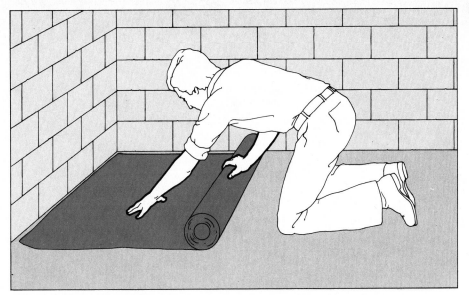

Waterproofing the slab. When a concrete slab is used as the base for sleepers, subfloor, underlayment and finish flooring, it need not be level but it must be dry. To waterproof the surface, first apply a ¼-inch-thick coating of roofing-type asphalt, available in 5-gallon cans at lumberyards or building-supply stores; use a stiff broom to coat the slab. Across the asphalt, stretch roofing paper in the 50- to 65-pound classification, available in 36-foot rolls. Press the paper down evenly and firmly until it lies flat over the asphalt.

Supports for a Subfloor

Reinforcing an attic floor. If the joists already in your attic are made of lumber smaller than 2-by-8, you will need to double the existing joists. Cut new pieces the same size and length and rest them on the 2-by-4 plates that run the length of the attic where joists and rafters meet. Nail them, using 16-penny nails, to the sides of the existing ones at several points along their lengths; toenail the ends to the plates. If joists are spaced more than 16 inches apart, add extras in between. Cut additional joists the same size and length as existing ones. Insert new joists between the existing ones, resting them on the plates, and toenail into place. If new joists do not match dimensions of the existing ones (a new 2-by-8, for example, may be ½ to ¾ inch smaller than an old one), use wood scraps under both ends of the new joist to make sure joist tops are flush.

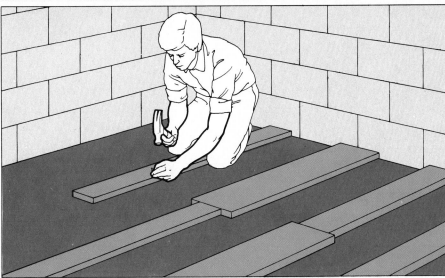

Sleepers for a slab. To provide the base for a floor in a basement or garage lay 2-by-4s flat across the planned room area at 16-inch intervals, measured from center to center. You need not buy new lumber to fabricate sleepers—any spare 2-inch lumber in your workshop will do. Whatever lumber you use, paint it with a wood preservative. Pound 2-inch concrete nails through the 2-by-4s, roofing paper and asphalt waterproofing layer, using only as many nails as needed to keep the sleepers from shifting until the subfloor is in place. If you want additional insulation—the air space probably affords enough—use batts between the sleepers, being careful to staple them with the vapor-barrier side up.

Subfloor and Underlayment

If you are adding a new subfloor, remember to install it before walls are put up, since the walls might prevent you from nailing the subfloor edges to the joists (and because you need something to stand on while building walls). Add the underlayment and the finish flooring after walls are in place.

Plywood makes an excellent subfloor material. In ⅝-inch thicknesses, it supplies a strong platform and virtually guarantees a squeakproof floor. Furthermore, the standard 4-by-8 sheets are easier to install than the various types of wood boards that are also used for subfloor materials. Grade C-D is commonly used; the C-grade side—a smoother finish—should face upward. To obtain maximum strength from a plywood subfloor, make sure the ends of adjacent sheets are not fastened to the same joist. Leave ¹⁄₁₆-inch spaces between the ends of the sheets and ⅛-inch spaces at the sides to permit the wood to expand without buckling; double these intervals in a room subject to high humidity.

After installation, some leveling of the subfloor may be necessary, but the underlayment will smooth out any minor unevenness. The underlayment also prevents damage from nails forced upward by movement of joists as they settle, expand or contract.

In kitchens, bathrooms and other areas that may be wet, the underlayment should be ¼-inch grade A-C plywood, which does not readily soak up moisture. The grade-A side should face upward. Elsewhere, use 4-by-4 squares of untempered hardboard, very smooth on one side but rough on the other, to hold the finish-flooring adhesive. With plywood, surface texture does not markedly affect the holding power of adhesives. Since hardboard is highly absorbent, do not allow it to become wet. Before installation, unwrap the sheets and stack them loosely against the walls of the new room for 24 hours to adjust to the normal humidity of the room; they will expand or contract slightly, but thereafter hold their shape. The rows of underlayment are laid perpendicular to those of the subfloor. If you use nails, screws or staples instead of adhesive (box, opposite) to fasten the underlayment to the subfloor, be sure the fasteners do not penetrate the joists. Otherwise, like the subfloor nails, they may be forced upward by joist movement to mar the finish flooring.

Installing the subfloor. Before starting to cut and lay the subfloor sheets, work out a pattern that avoids alignment of joints while requiring a minimum of plywood. Use full sheets, untrimmed, as much as possible. Lay the first row flush with any existing wall, and cut the last row to fit. Fasten the plywood to joists with coated No. 8 box nails. At the ends of the sheets, space the nails 6 inches apart and ⅜ inch from the edges. Stagger nails at adjoining ends to keep from splitting the joist. Between the ends of the sheets, space the nails 10 inches apart.

Smooth small bumps in the surface of the subfloor with rough sandpaper, and fill holes with flash patch (page 60). Unusually high places may be a result of swelling of joists; if so, pry the plywood up, level the joists with a plane and nail the sheets back.

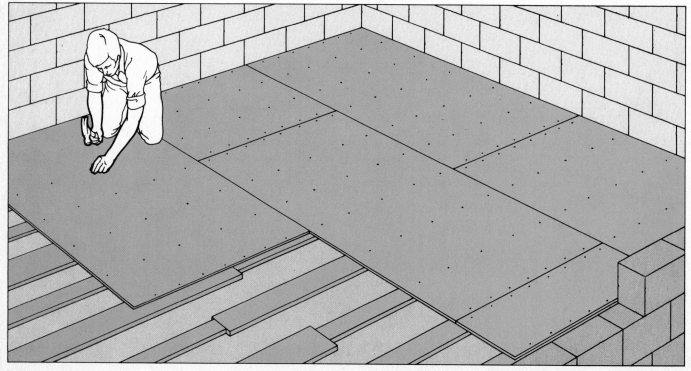

Installing the underlayment. Hardboard or plywood underlayment (*dark lines in the drawing below*) must be laid so that it always spans the subfloor joints (*light lines*) and, like the subfloor, it must be arranged in a staggered pattern. If you lay the subfloor before erecting walls and install the underlayment afterward—as you should—this overlapping is almost automatic, since the underlayment sheets will be offset from the subfloor by the thickness of the walls. Place underlayment sheets—rough surface up, in the case of hardboard—⅛ inch from walls; separate the sheets from each other by ¹⁄₃₂ inch, the thickness of a matchbook cover. To fit the last sheet in each row, follow the procedure used for border tiles, as shown on page 66. Unless underlayment sheets will be cemented down (*box, below*), fasteners should be spaced 4 inches apart over the entire board and ⅜ inch in from the edges. If necessary, mark off the surface in 4-inch squares as a guide.

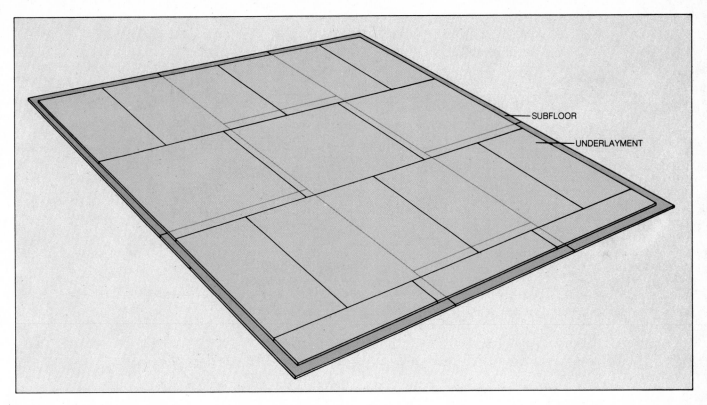

SUBFLOOR

UNDERLAYMENT

Four Fastening Methods

Underlayment can be attached to the subfloor in a variety of ways. They all work, but some work better—or save more time—than others.

☐ COATED BOX NAILS, well suited to the task, have a sheathing of resin that is melted by friction during driving and then rehardens to hold the nails firmly in place. The nails also have thin heads that will sink flush with the surface (ordinary headed nails would create lumps that might show through resilient tile). You can also use special underlayment nails, which have large but very thin heads that can be hammered flush with the surface; in the event of a mis-hit they are easier to pull out than coated nails.

☐ SCREWS can be sunk flush with the surface of the underlayment and will stay put. However, this method of fastening is extremely time consuming, given the number of screws and screw holes needed for just one sheet.

☐ STAPLES are used by most professional builders. This technique is fast and, if done correctly, leaves no telltale lumps on the underlayment surface. The heavy-duty staples required for the job are driven by a stapler known as a power nailer—available at tool-rental agencies. Get some practice with waste board first, since it is easy to drive staples either too far into the surface, or not far enough, or sideways.

☐ ADHESIVE, applied to the subfloor, is also used by many contractors to affix underlayment. A special type, known simply as construction adhesive, is used for the job. If the underlayment is hardboard, roughen the downward-facing surface with coarse sandpaper to create the texture needed for firm sticking.

Laying Tile to Finish the Floor

Tile is a serviceable and handsome flooring for any remodeled room. It can be made of ceramic, cork, asphalt, wood or vinyl that has been impregnated with asbestos fibers. All types of tile are set down in much the same way, although there may be some minor differences cementing them in place and cutting them for borders. On these pages and overleaf, the basic tile-laying process is described as it applies to vinyl asbestos, one of the most popular tile materials. With only slight variations, the same system serves for another popular tile—wood block *(page 67)*.

No matter what the material, write down the dimensions of your room, so that your building-supply dealer can compute the amount of tile required (such calculations are simple for 1-foot-square tiles, the most common size, since the area in square feet is the number of tiles needed). To allow for errors and odd spaces, buy enough extra tile to run the length of the long wall.

Both vinyl asbestos and wood-block tiles come in self-sticking versions, with adhesive on the underside beneath backing paper. However, this layer of glue is thin, and you can achieve a better bond by using dry tiles that are laid in adhesive applied to the underlayment. Ask your dealer for the correct adhesive.

Tile should be laid in a pyramid pattern over half the floor at a time; this method helps ensure straight rows and snug fits, since you will always have guidance on two sides when putting the tiles in place. The starting point for most tile pyramids is set with the aid of a chalk line to avoid having to cut narrow strips for borders; for some tiles, the starting point is the center of areas subject to heavy traffic.

If you are laying adhesive-backed tiles on hardboard underlayment, brush wood sealer over the hardboard and allow it to dry to the touch; the sealer will keep the tile's thin layer of glue from being soaked up by the absorbent hardboard. If you use dry tiles, cover half the room with adhesive, starting at one wall; then lay tiles from the center of the room, crouching or kneeling on those already in place. Repeat the process for the other half.

A Dry Run to Find the Starting Point

1 **Lining up the tiles.** Chalk a length of string and tie it tautly between nails set in the exact middle of opposite walls of the room. Without snapping the string, place a tile at the approximate center of the line with its edge on the string bisecting the room. From this starting point lay a row of dry tile to the wall, perpendicular to the line. If the last tile in the row leaves a space of 2 inches or more to the wall, proceed to Step 2. If there is less than a 2-inch space, move the row so the last tile is ⅛ inch from the wall. This ensures that tiles will be even at borders.

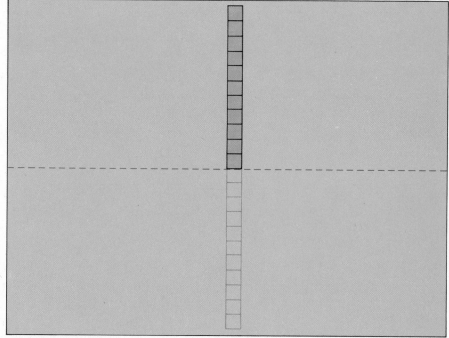

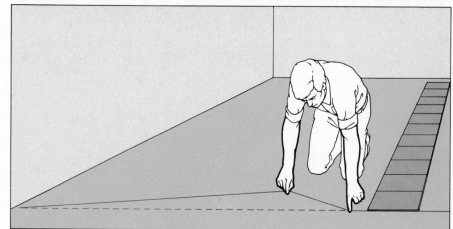

2 **Marking the first chalk line.** Align the chalked string so that it runs along the edge of the first tile in the row, moving the string if necessary. Press down on the chalked string in the middle of the room. Snap one side of the string and then the other so that a chalk line is deposited.

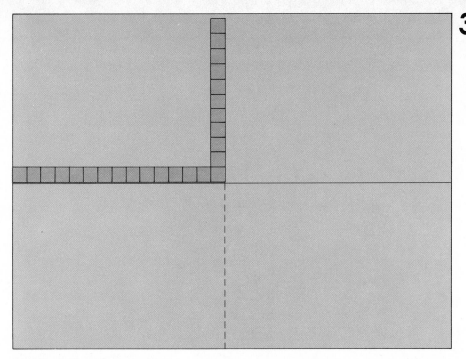

3 **Marking a perpendicular line.** Place a second row of tiles perpendicular to the first, with the row's edge on the chalk line (*solid line*). If the last tile in the new row leaves a space of less than 2 inches to the wall, slide both the new row and the first row toward that wall until the last tile is ⅛ inch from the wall. Snap another chalk line (*dotted line*) along the edge of the first row. Then remove all the tiles.

Placing the Tiles

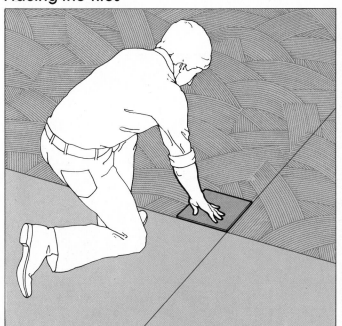

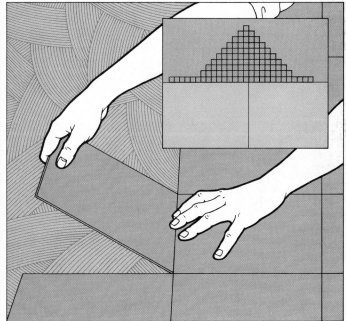

1 **Starting the pyramid.** If you are using adhesive-backed tiles, strip the backing paper off the undersides and lay the tiles directly on the underlayment, beginning at the right angles formed by the intersection of the chalk lines in the middle of the room.

For dry tiles, first spread adhesive over half the room at a time with a notched trowel, starting at the walls and working back down to the center of the room. Take care not to cover the chalk lines. As with adhesive-backed tiles, begin laying the tiles at the chalk-line intersection.

2 **The emplacement technique.** As you lay tiles in a pyramid pattern (*inset*), butt each new tile against an edge of one already laid and drop the new tile in place; sliding it into position will force adhesive up and onto the tile's surface.

Custom Cuts for Borders

Cutting tiles for borders. Place a tile squarely over the fixed tile closest to the border. Hold a second tile over it ⅛ inch from the wall. Using the second tile's edge as a guide, score the first tile with a linoleum knife. Snap the scored tile. One piece will just fit into the border area.

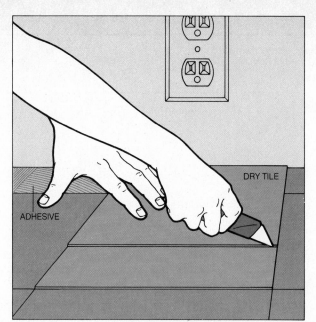

Cutting tile for corners. Place a tile squarely over the last fixed tile on the left side of the corner. Hold a second tile over the first ⅛ inch from the border. Using the second tile's edge as a guide, mark the first with a pencil (*below*). Next move the first tile, without turning it, to a position squarely over the fixed tile closest to the right side of the border (*below, right*). Again using an overlying tile as your guide, make a second pencil line. Cut the marked tile along the pencil lines and fit it into the corner.

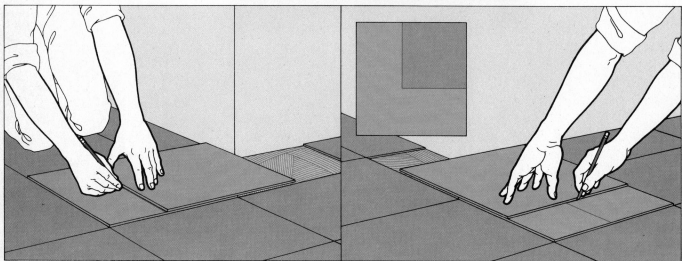

Fitting tile to irregular areas. This is done in much the same way as shaping tile for borders. Move the top tile along the irregular length of wall—in this case an ornate doorjamb—so that each of its corners fits successive surfaces. With each change of position, mark the underlying tile. Here, for example, the marks in the drawings at right correspond to similarly designated portions of the doorjamb. If there is a curved area, bend a piece of wire—wire solder is ideal if you have some in your workshop—to transfer the curve to the tile being fitted as in the drawing at far right. Connect the various marks, cut through the tile with a linoleum knife and fit it into position.

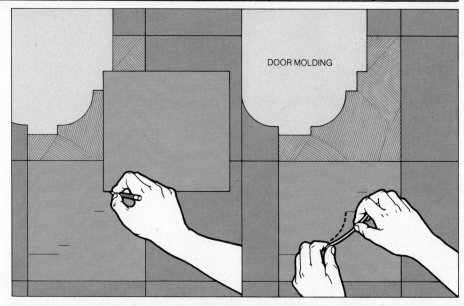

Shortcut to a Hardwood Floor

Wood-block, or parquet, flooring provides a hardwood finish without requiring the finicky work of nailing, sanding and sealing wood boards. The square blocks, made of glued layers or strips of prefinished oak or other hardwoods, come in numerous sizes and patterns.

Like vinyl-asbestos tiles, wood block is available in both dry and self-sticking versions, and it is installed in basically the same fashion—with a few variations. For one thing whole blocks are placed through doorways or heavy-traffic areas; this is necessary because glue will stand up best under constant stress if under a full-sized block. The glue itself is different from that used on other tile: wood block requires mastic, a more viscous substance than standard tile adhesive. Some blocks also have an interlocking tongue-and-groove feature to help hold them in place.

Wood blocks also absorb moisture; let them stand loosely in the room for 72 hours to adjust to humidity levels or they will buckle after installation.

If the room next to the newly finished wood-block floor has carpeting that projects into the threshold between rooms, fold the carpet under itself until it is flush with the wood block and tack it down with carpet tacks. If the carpet does not project into the threshold, or if the adjacent room is covered with wood strip or resilient tile, a metal strip, called a transitional threshold, must be used to ensure a smooth—and safe—joint.

2 **Laying the blocks.** Spread a layer of mastic ⅛ inch thick over half the room, using a notched trowel. Lay wood blocks in a pyramid pattern, as described in Step 2 on page 65. With tongue-and-groove wood block, press the squares together, then place a block of wood at each edge and tap it gently with a mallet to ensure a tight fit. An extra square of parquet is ideal for this, but be sure to fit tongue against tongue and groove against groove before using the mallet.

Fit blocks at borders and around doorways, using the techniques described on the opposite page. Mark with a pencil rather than a knife. Cut along the lines with a 10-point saw.

1 **Marking the chalk lines.** Begin a row of loose blocks in the center of a doorway with the first block set completely through the threshold (*inset*). Lay tile to the middle of the room. If there is no other door, mark a chalk line perpendicular to the row, using the edge of the last block as your guide; then lay a second row along that line and snap a chalk line perpendicular to the first one (i.e., alongside the first row).

If there is another doorway in an adjoining wall (*below*), lay the second row of blocks from the center of, and through, the threshold to the middle of the room. Shift the rows so the last block in one row aligns with the last block in the other. Snap the second chalk line along the side of the first row. Remove the blocks.

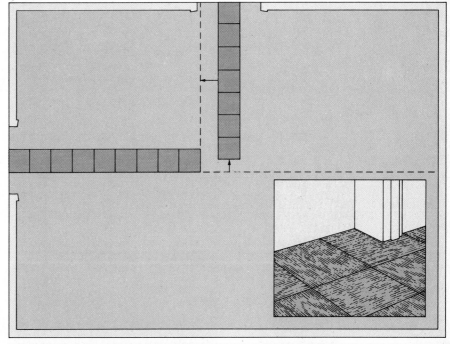

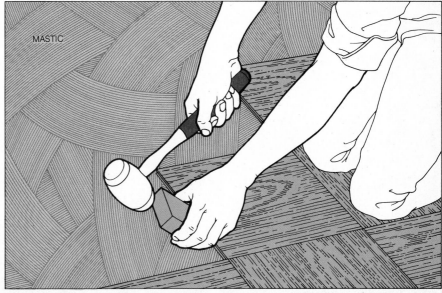

MASTIC

Building a Ceiling from Frame to Finish

When a ceiling is added to a new living space most people finish it with acoustical tiles, acoustical panels or gypsum wallboard. All require an overhead support framework. If no joist framework exists, one can be built.

Wallboard is least expensive and most adaptable to different decorative treatments. Acoustical tiles or panels are simpler to install in some cases, and their sound-absorbing qualities are often very useful. Both tiles and panels are easily marred—a fact to consider in planning the ceiling of a playroom or any low-beamed room—and repainting them is more difficult than refinishing wallboard.

Acoustical tiles can be installed on an unfinished ceiling (or on one in poor condition) by stapling them to a grid of furring strips nailed across joists, but often it is easier to suspend a grid of aluminum strips and place acoustical panels in them. A suspended ceiling may be best if you wish to lower the ceiling, or if you need to cover pipes and ducts extending below the joists. A suspended ceiling with removable panels also allows great flexibility in installing overhead lights and permits access to hidden fixtures such as shutoff valves in water lines. Dealers sell complete suspended-ceiling packages that include both acoustical panels and the metal supports.

Installing wallboard requires more labor than hanging a suspended ceiling. You will need at least one other person to help get the heavy panels into place while you nail them up. And you must work overhead to nail and cement joints.

Preparing Collar Beams for an Attic

1 Measuring and marking. On a rafter near the end wall of the attic, mark the height of your proposed ceiling. A good ceiling height is 7½ feet but lower ceilings are adequate and attractive if you feel that the room will have enough headroom, light and ventilation. To ensure the consistent and accurate measurements essential to building a level ceiling, cut a length of scrap lumber as long as the proposed ceiling height. Stand it upright against a rafter, using a level to make sure it is vertical, and mark the rafter where it and the top of the board intersect. Similarly mark the rafter immediately opposite.

Farther down on the same two rafters, locate the top of your knee wall. A knee wall 5 feet high is adequate for general use; low furniture—a bunk bed or a storage chest—will fit comfortably against even a 4-foot-high knee wall.

2 **Making a pattern.** Collar beams of 2-by-6-inch lumber nailed to the rafters will support the attic ceiling. Determine the length of the beams by measuring from the outside edge of one rafter to the outside edge of the opposite rafter at the proposed ceiling height. Bevel the ends of each beam before installing it. The beveled ends offer maximum nailing surface, with less risk of splitting a beam end. Make a pattern for the bevel from a square of cardboard tacked to a rafter, placing one edge flush with the outside edge of the rafter. Hold a level against the square with one corner of the level at the outermost corner of the square. From this corner draw a horizontal line. Detach the square, cut along the line and discard the lower portion. On both sides of the remaining piece, mark with chalk along both the newly cut edge and the edge that was tacked flush with the rafter edge. The angle formed by these two edges is the bevel angle. If the pitch of the opposite roof is at a different angle, make an additional pattern.

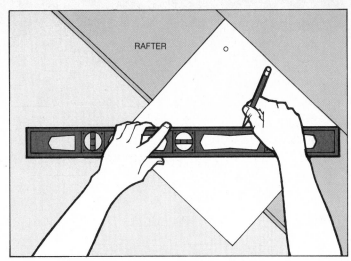

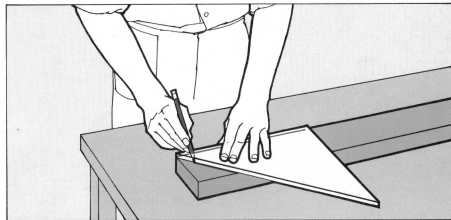

3 **Trimming the beams.** Place the apex of the angle formed by the two chalked edges of the pattern at one end of a collar beam. Hold either one of the pattern's two chalked edges flush with the bottom edge of the beam. Draw a pencil line along the other chalked edge of the pattern. Similarly, mark the other end of the beam. Cut off the ends of the beam by sawing about ¼ inch inside these two diagonal marks.

Nailing In the Beams

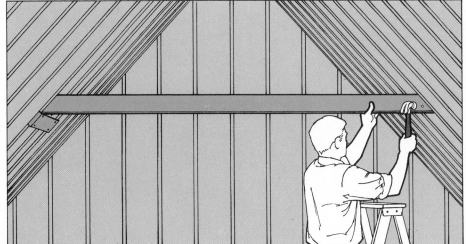

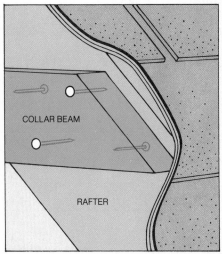

1 **Positioning the beams.** Snap a chalk line at ceiling height across the rafters on each side of the attic. Temporarily fasten a 1-by-3-inch support board across two or three rafters, just below the chalk line, driving nails partway. Drive one tenpenny nail into each end of a collar beam. Rest one end of the beam on the support board next to a rafter. Position the

other end of the beam against the opposite rafter with the beam's bottom edge at ceiling height, as indicated by the chalk mark. Drive the two nails partway into the two rafters. Check the beam with a level. If it is not horizontal, recheck the ceiling height measurements on both rafters, adjust the beam until it is level, then nail it in place (Step 2, right).

2 **Fastening the beams.** Drive two tenpenny nails through the beam and into the rafter. Then, working from the other side of the rafter, drive two more nails through the rafter and into the beam. This helps to avoid splitting the beam. Install the remaining beams in the same way.

Suspending a Ceiling

Suspended ceilings are usually made of 2-foot-by-4-foot acoustical panels supported by a metal grid. This framework consists of long main runners connected at 4-foot intervals by 2-foot cross Ts. The runners are usually hung at right angles to the joists and are held up by hanger wires attached to the bottom edges of the joists. The outer edges of the ceiling are supported by edge framing, which is L shaped in cross section and which is attached to the walls with the vertical stroke of the L uppermost.

Both the hardware—framing, runners, and hanger wires—and the acoustical panels are adaptable to all room sizes and designs. Runners, sold in 8-, 10- or 12-foot lengths, are made of light aluminum sheet metal that can be cut to fit with tin shears. Tabs at the ends interlink and lock to extend the length. Holes for hanger wires occur every 3 inches, and slots for cross Ts every 6 inches. Edge framing is flexible enough to accommodate slight irregularities in wall surfaces. Trim the panels with a utility knife.

1 **Measuring ceiling height.** Mark the proposed ceiling height—allowing room below the joists to clear ducts, pipes or other obstructions—on the wall at the corners of the room. In each corner drive a nail into a stud at the level marked. Stretch a chalk line tautly between the nails, and snap the line across each wall.

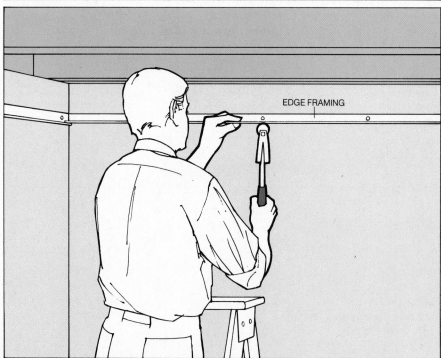

2 **Installing edge framing.** Screw or nail edge framing into studs along each wall at ceiling height. Where the ends of two strips of framing meet at a corner, lap one end over the other.

3 **Positioning runners and cross Ts.** To ensure a symmetrical arrangement of the panels, start by marking the centers of the walls at joist level. Since the short ends of the panels will abut the walls parallel to the joists, these walls must be divided into centered 2-foot intervals. Measure from center to corner, and determine the distance in inches beyond the last even number of feet. If this overage is 6 inches or more *(top right)*, snap a chalk line across the joist bottoms from the center of one wall to the center of the other. If the overage is less than 6 inches, mark the joists along a line a foot to one side or the other of the midpoints *(bottom right)*. In either case, mark across the joists at 2-foot intervals on both sides of the first line.

In centering the long dimension of the panels on the walls perpendicular to joists, measure in the same way from center to corner. The overage is the distance to the corner from the last 4-, 8- or 12-foot mark. If the overage is 6 inches or more *(top right)*, plan to space cross Ts at 4-foot intervals on both sides of the center mark. If the overage is less than 6 inches *(bottom right)*, space cross Ts from points 2 feet on either side of the center. Mark the walls above the edge framing for cross Ts.

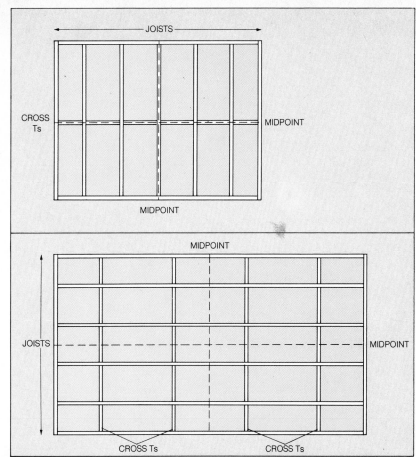

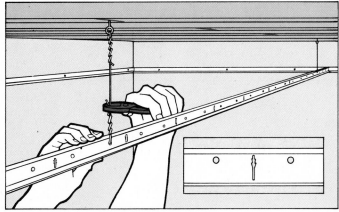

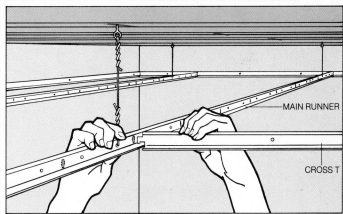

4 **Attaching runners.** Along the lines marked across the joists, attach an eye screw to the bottom edge of every other joist. Insert a hanger wire in each eye, secure the wires by twisting and bend the free ends to a 90° angle. Ensure alignment of the cross-T slots in the runners by stretching a line between center marks on the walls perpendicular to the joists. Hang the runners so that a T slot lies just above the string. Add lengths of runners as needed and cut off the excess. Set each runner in place with its ends resting on the edge framing. Thread hanger wires through the holes in the runners. Level each runner by adjusting the hanger wires, then secure each wire by twisting it around itself.

5 **Connecting the cross Ts.** Connect the runners with cross Ts at the proper intervals by fitting the ends of the cross Ts into the slots in the runners. Along the two walls perpendicular to the joists, rest the outer ends of the cross Ts on the edge framing.

Install panels in all the full-sized openings in the grid. Lift each panel diagonally up through the framework, turn it to the horizontal and rest its edges on the flanges of the runners and the cross Ts. Check the alignment of full-sized panels and grid, then trim panels to fit the smaller spaces around the border of the grid and install them.

Inserting a Fluorescent Light Fixture

Suspended ceilings offer a variety of opportunities for installing either fluorescent or incandescent light fixtures. The simplest method is to replace one full-sized panel with a troffer type of fixture,—one with a shallow rectangular reflector the same size as a panel.

Such a fixture usually comes with a light-diffusing screen of transparent plastic, and a receptacle for housing the connections to a power source. If the original ceiling fixture employed a hanging cord switch, you will have to install a wall switch for the troffer.

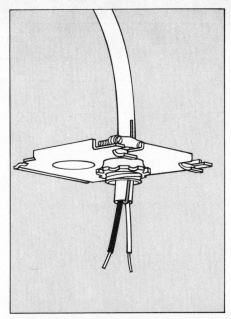

1 Connecting cable to cover plate. Knock out one of the punch holes in the cover plate from the light fixture, and insert the nozzle, or threaded end, of a cable connector through from the top, or ridged, side. Screw the nozzle nut tightly to hold the connector to the plate.

Cut 3 inches of sheathing off the end of a length of plastic-sheathed cable, wire size No. 14, and double back the bare copper ground wire along the cable. Peel off ¾ inch of insulation to bare the ends of the black and white wires. Slip these wires through the clamp on the connector and out the nozzle until a little of the cable sheathing comes through. With a screwdriver, tighten the cable clamp so that the half ring centers on the ground wire and grips it.

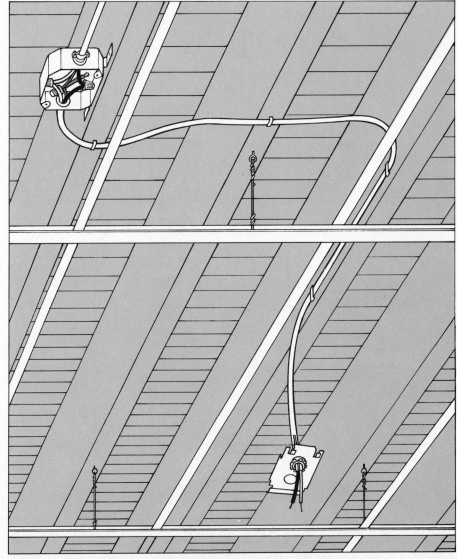

2 Running cable to a junction box. Cut the cable long enough to reach from where you want to place the light fixture to the junction box that holds the original ceiling light. Turn off the current at the service panel. Unscrew the original fixture from the box; disconnect and straighten wires. Fasten the cable to the junction box with another cable connector, but in this case attach the ground wire to the box with a screw. Connect the wires from the power source and from the fixture with wire nuts, white to white and black to black. Screw a cover plate to the box.

With insulated cable staples, fasten the cable to the joists, but leave the plate-connected end dangling at the fixture position on the grid.

72

3 **Putting up the fixture.** Leave the grid openings surrounding the fixture empty in order to have ample space to work in. With the help of a partner if necessary, angle the fixture into place and set it on the grid.

4 **Connecting cable to fixture wires.** Wire-nut both white wires from the light fixture to the white wire of the cable. Wire-nut both black wires from the fixture to the black wire of the cable. Then push the wiring into the opening on the fixture and attach the cover plate. Slide the tail of the plate under one edge of the opening, then push it in the other direction until the nose lugs engage and it locks. Staple the cable at one more point if it seems floppy. Restore the power.

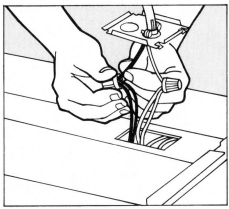

Providing a Wall Switch

1 **Making connections in the junction box.** If the original ceiling light used a pull cord as a switch, you will have to install a wall switch for the new fixture. Buy a switch with a green screw terminal for the cable's bare ground wire.

From the wall near an entry door to a knockout hole in the ceiling junction box, run No. 14 cable. Staple the cable to the joists at 4-foot intervals and at bends. Disconnect the current. In the ceiling junction box, join the white wire of the power source to the white wire of the cable from the new light fixture. Join the black wire from the switch to the black wire from the fixture. Mark the white wire from the switch with black paint or tape (to show that it is a hot wire in this application), and join it to the black hot wire from the power source. Wire-nut the three bare ground wires together and connect them with green wire to the grounding screw. Cover the box with a plate.

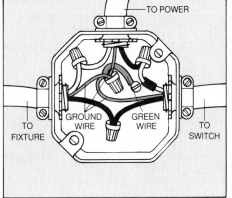

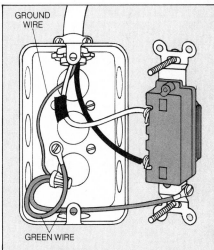

2 **Connecting the wall switch.** At the wall, run the cable into a standard outlet box. Connect the bare ground wire with green wires leading to grounding terminals in the box and on the switch. Connect the black and white wires to the terminal screws. Mark or paint the white wire—again, to show that it is hot. Screw the switch to the wall and turn on the power.

Putting Up a Tile Ceiling

1 Planning the job. Acoustical tiles, 12 inches by 12 inches, make a suitable ceiling for a new living space in a basement, attic or unfinished room. At ceiling level, make chalk marks at the centers of all four walls. Measure from each mark to an adjacent corner. This distance will be a number of feet plus, usually, a fraction of a foot. If the fraction is less than 3 inches, move the center markers 6 inches right or left. Mark 12-inch intervals from the center markers to the adjoining walls. To determine how many 1-by-3 furring strips you need, count the number of marks on one of the walls parallel to the joists and add two extra. Cut each strip the length of the walls perpendicular to the joists. To estimate the number of tiles required, count the number of 12-inch intervals on two adjoining walls; add one to each of these figures and multiply them.

Any extensive electrical wiring that is to be installed in the room should be completed before you put up the furring.

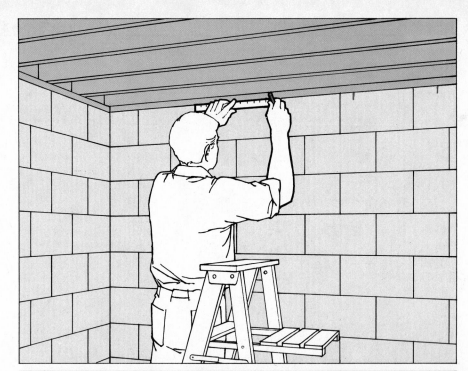

Holding the Edge

Where you find a gap between the end joist and the wall, supply a nailing surface for the ends of the furring strips by adding a false joist. Cut a 2-by-4 or 2-by-6 just enough shorter than a joist so that you can raise it to rest flat on the side sill plate at one end, and then slide it over to rest on the sill at the other end. Cut 1-by-3s to a length equal to the width of a joist. Every 2 or 3 feet nail these segments—called kickers—to the outer edge of the false joist, with their upper ends against the subfloor. Position the joist's inner edge to lie where the furring strips will end. The kickers provide solid nailing for the strips, which in turn hold the joist in place.

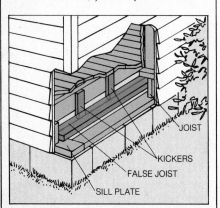

JOIST
KICKERS
FALSE JOIST
SILL PLATE

2 Putting up furring strips. Tape a carpenter's level to the narrow side of a straight 2-by-4 and check the joists lengthwise and crosswise to see how level a base they will provide. If they vary sharply, start by holding the first strip at right angles to the joists at their lowest level. Center the ends between the nearest pair of chalk marks and attach the strip to the joist with an eightpenny nail. Using a level to guide you, shim the rest of the strip down from the high joists. Level the other strips from the first one, attaching a strip between each remaining pair of chalk marks and against the end walls.

3 **Adjusting ceiling fixtures.** If a furring strip crosses an existing ceiling fixture, you must disconnect the fixture. Turn off the electric circuit. Remove the screws or nuts holding the fixture in place, pull it away from the box and disconnect the wires. Detach the ceiling box from the joist or loosen it from the hanger and slide it back along the cable out of the way of the strip. Reattach the box, lowering it if necessary so the bottom rim will be flush with the ceiling when the tiles are installed. Leave the power off.

4 **Putting up the first tile.** Snap a chalk line down the center of the next-to-last furring strip on one side of the room and another line—intersecting the first at right angles—between the last pair of chalk marks at one end of the room. Set the tile in the corner where the lines intersect with the raised, or tongue, edges toward the corner and the stapling flanges toward the center of the room. Align the finished rims with the chalk marks. Staple both ends of the flanges on the grooved edges to the furring strips.

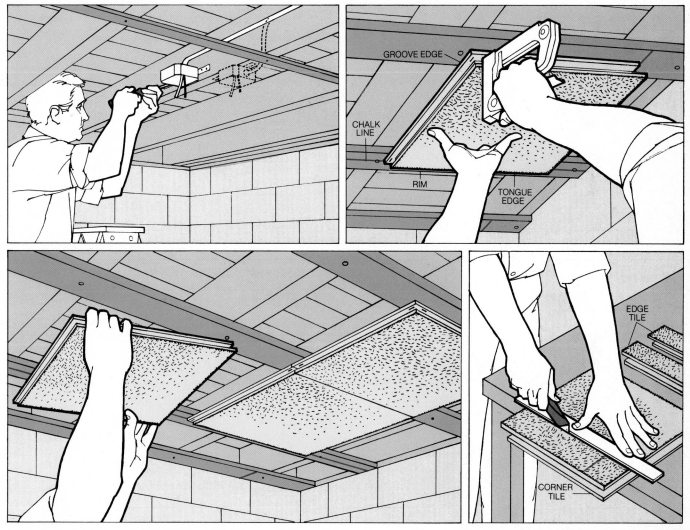

5 **Attaching adjacent tiles.** With the adjoining raised edges toward the corner, slide the tongue of the next tile into the groove on the stapled edge of the preceding tile. Align the rims of the new tile with the chalk line or the rims of the preceding one. Then staple the flanges on the projecting grooved edges of the new tile to the furring strips.

6 **Adding border tiles.** After installing three tiles, measure the distance from their outer rims to the walls at both ends of each tile. Deduct ¼ inch from each measurement and use the results to mark the required sizes for the corner and edge tiles. Be sure to measure from the rims along the grooved edges. Draw lines between the marks and cut the tiles with a utility knife. Slide the pieces into place, starting with the corner tile, and anchor them to the furring strips with 1½-inch common nails.

7 **Marking the site of an outlet box.** Before you reach the area where you must tile around the outlet box of a ceiling fixture, remove the fixture and relocate the box *(page 75, Step 3)*, if you have not already done so. Reattach the box to a joist so that it will be more or less in the middle of a tile and so that its lower rim will be flush with the surface of the ceiling. Tile as closely as possible to two adjacent sides of the relocated box, then slip the tongue of a fresh tile into the groove of a tile already installed on one side of the box. Slide the loose tile up to the box and mark the tongue of the tile at the point where it touches the midpoint of the rim of the box, but do not mark the face of the tile. Slide the same tile up to the adjoining side of the box and mark the point on the tile's other tongue where it touches the midpoint of the rim.

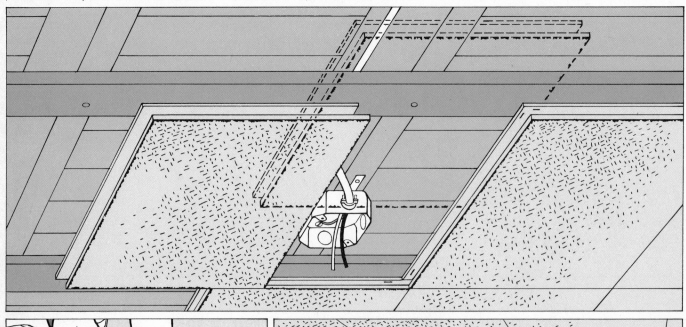

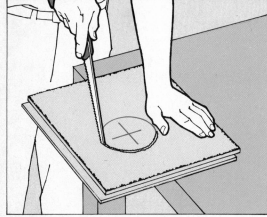

8 **Trimming the tile.** Using an L square, extend the marks on the tongues of the tile. The point at which these lines intersect on the back of the tile marks the center of the outlet box. Transfer the center mark to the face of the tile. Set a compass to a measure slightly less than half the distance from rim to rim of the box at its longest dimension. Draw a circle of this radius on the face of the tile with the center of the circle at the point of intersection of the two lines. Using a keyhole saw held with the blade pointed outward at a slight angle, make a beveled cut around the circle through the face to the back of the tile. Staple the tile in place around the box as described on page 75, Step 5. Then reattach the fixture and turn the circuit back on.

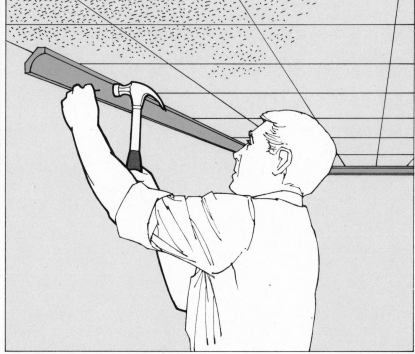

9 **Finishing the ceiling.** After installing all the tiles, use the procedure on pages 46-47 to cope-joint 1½-inch cove molding to cover the line between walls and ceiling. Attach the molding as described on pages 48-49.

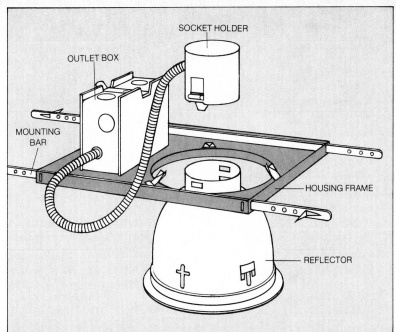

SOCKET HOLDER

OUTLET BOX

MOUNTING BAR

HOUSING FRAME

REFLECTOR

Recessing a Light Fixture

1 **Selecting the fixture.** Buy a recessed fixture that is prewired to its own outlet box and is equipped with a reflector that fits into a round receptacle. If there was a previous fixture, connect the new outlet box to the old circuit; otherwise, extend the house wiring to the desired location of the new fixture.

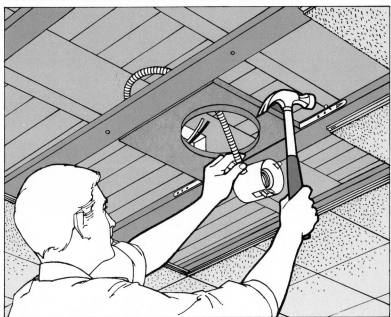

2 **Installing the housing frame.** Tile the ceiling to a point near the approximate location selected for the fixture. Hold in place, but do not fasten, the tile that will come under the fixture. Mark its boundaries, remove it and position the housing frame of the fixture between two furring strips so the center of the frame will be more or less above the center of the tile.

Fasten the housing frame to the edges of adjoining furring strips by driving nails into the furring strips through the holes in the mounting bars attached to two sides of the housing frame. The bottom of the housing frame should be flush with the bottom of the furring strips. Connect the fixture to a power source.

3 **Completing the installation.** Using the method described in Steps 7 and 8 at left, determine the location of the center of the hole you will cut in the tile to accommodate the round receptacle in the bottom of the housing frame. Cut the hole and install the tile. After you finish tiling around the fixture, snap the reflector-trim unit into the socket holder. Insert a bulb of the size specified by the manufacturer, and push the reflector-trim unit up into the receptacle at the bottom of the housing frame.

Special Techniques for a Wallboard Ceiling

1 Planning a wallboard ceiling. Cover the ceiling before the walls, measuring ceiling dimensions from top plate of one wall to top plate of another. Install sheets perpendicular to the joists. Diagram the ceiling, keeping in mind several principles: the ends of the wallboard must be made to land on the center lines of joists, by trimming the board if necessary; these joints must be staggered to prevent a continuous seam on a single joist; any filler strips of wallboard should be installed in the center of the ceiling for convenience in taping joints.

Where room dimensions create a narrow gap between the edge of a sheet and the wall, as in the ell, 4 feet, 4 inches deep, shown at right, trim back the sheet to widen the gap to at least 1 foot, and cut a piece to fill it.

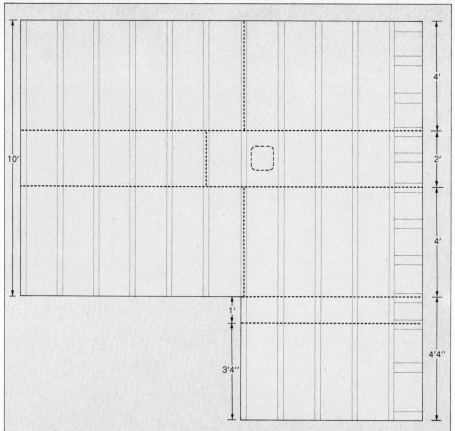

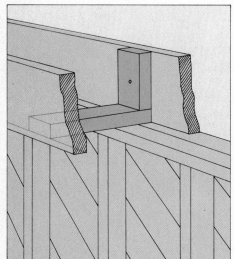

2 Providing nailing surfaces. If the joist adjacent and parallel to a wall lies more than 4 inches out from it, you must provide nailing blocks for the wallboard ends. Most such walls, typically the end walls of a house, carry a joist on top of the plate. Using 2-by-4 scraps and tenpenny nails, make L-shaped nailing blocks. The vertical members should be 1½ inches shorter than the width of the joists. Horizontal members should be as long as the distance between the wall-top joist and its neighbor. Position the Ls in corners and on 16-inch centers in between, adjusting to provide nailing surfaces where the wallboard corners join. One nail will hold the upright to the wall-top joist, another nail will secure the other end of the horizontal.

If the wall is an interior wall, cut blocks 14½ inches long, lay them at right angles across the top of the plate, and nail into each end through the joists that the blocks abut.

3 Marking guidelines for nails. Make a vertical mark on the plates below the center of each joist end, and beneath the nailing blocks if you have any. The marks will establish the sight lines your wallboard nails must follow after the wallboard hides the joist itself.

4 Applying adhesive to joints. Use glue in fastening ceilings; it will reduce the number of nails that must be driven from an awkward position and that will require covering with compound later on. With a caulking gun, lay straight beads of wallboard panel adhesive along joists that will touch wallboard. On joists where panels join, zigzag the adhesive so that both edges will stick.

5 **Putting up wallboard.** Start in a corner and butt the sheets in a continuous line. Get someone to help you lift the wallboard, which is too heavy for one person to handle. Make a T brace the height of your ceiling for your assistant to use in holding up the sheet while you nail. When you have the end of a sheet centered on the joist where it will join the next sheet, push the first nails into the board ½ inch from the edge at 16-inch intervals. Standard 1⅜-inch ring-shank wallboard nails are made sharp enough to penetrate the board. To drive them home, try the position professional wallboard hangers use. Hold the hammer in front of your face, with your thumb against the handle, and hit the nails by rotating your wrist and forearm (*insert*).

6 **Nailing and fitting.** Nail at 16-inch intervals, both around the wallboard edges and along the joist lines. Dimple the board around each nail as described on page 38, Step 2. To cut short or narrow pieces, score and break as shown on page 36. Measure and cut for corners in the manner shown on page 38, Step 3.

When it becomes obvious that the next sheet of wallboard will require an opening for lighting or ventilation, measure from the closest edges of mounted wallboard to the fixture or air duct. Use these measurements to outline the aperture on the wallboard, and cut with a keyhole saw pushed through a starter slit made with a utility knife. Finish the joints between panels with joint compound and tape (*pages 40-41*). Similarly fill the dimples with joint compound.

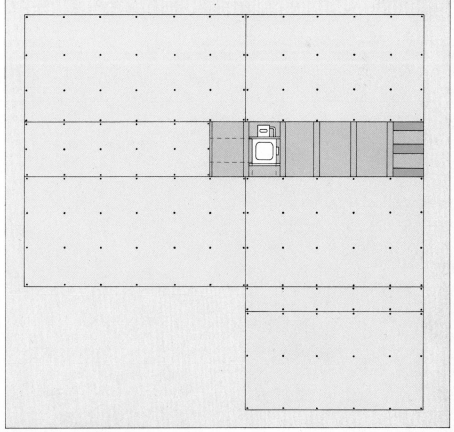

4

Bringing In the Out-of-Doors

Getting at a view. A prehung window, already glazed for looking at the outdoors and lighting the indoors, can go straight from the lumberyard into a framed opening in the house wall. Adding the frame to an existing wall or building it into a new one calls for only simple carpentry, readily accomplished with familiar power and hand tools such as a circular saw and a hammer.

A variant of Parkinson's law decrees that family living expands to fill available space. A darkroom claims squatter's rights to the unused corner of the basement; the attic is finished as an extra bedroom; the living room is partitioned to separate a dining area. Further expansion then depends on enclosing outdoor space. Adding a deck that opens from the kitchen or family room *(pages 120-125)* provides a new arena for entertaining, barbecuing, dining or lounging during the warm months. And enclosing a porch, covered patio, breezeway or garage *(pages 106-111 and 114-119)* produces a breakfast room or family activity room that can be used year round.

Enclosing an existing structure is far simpler than building an addition to the house from scratch—the heavy work of providing roof, foundation and supports has already been done for you. Flooring over the concrete slab of a breezeway or garage is like adding a wood floor to a basement. And putting up exterior walls calls for many of the framing techniques used for interior partitions.

Exterior walls are, however, more complicated than interior partitions. They need fire stops—crosspieces designed to block flame. They must be sheathed against the elements with plywood or fiberboard and siding, and lined with insulating batts or blankets *(pages 102-103)*. The ceiling in a new enclosure also needs similar insulation—in full sun the surface of a roof can reach 160°.

Porch or garage conversions usually entail installing doors and windows in existing house walls, in the new exterior ones or in both. If the new enclosure surrounds an existing back door, you may have to add another exit. Including rough openings for doors and windows in the new exterior framing is no trickier than allowing for a door in an interior partition. And turning an existing window opening on a frame house into a doorway *(pages 82-87)* is almost as easy. Breaking through existing walls and adding new studs and headers *(pages 88-91)* takes more time and energy, but even cutting into masonry walls requires less special skill than patience.

Once the opening is readied, the work of actually installing a door *(pages 86-87)* or window *(pages 98-101)* goes fast—thanks to factory-assembled units. Carpenters used to construct windows from scratch, a job that involved joining no fewer than 18 differently named parts for a simple double-hung window. Ensuring the smooth operation of a door was so tricky that master builders once breathed on the hinges before mortising them to invoke an auspicious outcome. Now doors and windows come prehung, with all their operating parts fixed in a finished jamb that needs only to be positioned and secured. And the task of expanding the house becomes mainly one of adapting pieces off a production line so they fit together.

The Trick of Converting a Window to a Door

Adding a new exterior door or window to your house is easier than it sounds. Even making a hole in the wall can be fairly simple if the exterior is wood, aluminum or stucco. Cutting through masonry, of course, is heavier work *(pages 92-97)*. But both the door and the window units come ready-assembled in a wide variety of styles and sizes so that no finicky carpentry is involved in installing them.

The quickest way to add a new door to a frame house—one whose basic structure is made of wood studs, not of solid masonry—is to take out an existing window, lengthen the opening and put a door unit in its place. To take advantage of this simple method, you must be able to find for your door opening a window of suitable size; most ready-made doors are 6 feet, 8 inches high and 32 or 36 inches wide. Inside the window casing, measure the height from the underside of the top jamb to the floor and the width between the side jambs. You also need a window with no obstructions hidden in the wall beneath it; check rooms above and below for piping or cables. You may have to cut a hole and inspect the area.

Where you do not have a window of the appropriate size in the appropriate place—or if you wish to put in a window, not a door—you can do that, too, by making a new opening in the wall and framing it as shown on pages 90-91.

For a flush fit outside and inside with wood, aluminum or stucco, choose a door 4⅝ inches thick if your interior walls are wallboard, 5⅜ inches thick if they are plaster. For brick veneer or solid masonry, either thickness will serve because the door will be recessed flush with the interior wall.

Like prehung interior doors, the exterior models can be hinged on the right or left side. Unlike them, however, exterior doors do not have a split jamb with finished casing on both sides but come with a solid jamb that is trimmed only on the outside. You must assemble the interior trim after you install the unit *(page 86)*. On most doors, the exterior casing or brick mold is 2 inches wide and extends about 1½ inches beyond the jamb. When you are replacing a window with a door, you may need to order wider casing to make it match the size of the existing exterior trim.

Getting at the window. Before you can take the basic frame, or jamb, of a window out of a wall, you have to remove the trim and sashes piece by piece. The first pieces to go are the strips of interior casing around the window and the stop molding along the sides—and, sometimes, the top—of the jamb. Then comes the apron under the interior sill, or stool, and the sill piece itself. Next is the hardware that holds the glazed sashes.

On the standard double-hung window, shown separated from the trim in the drawing at left, this hardware consists of metal channels and springs. You need to take off the exterior casing to remove them completely. Other types of windows have sash cords or hinges. You can lift out the sashes from the inside and remove the exterior casing afterward; a little experimenting will show what you need to undo.

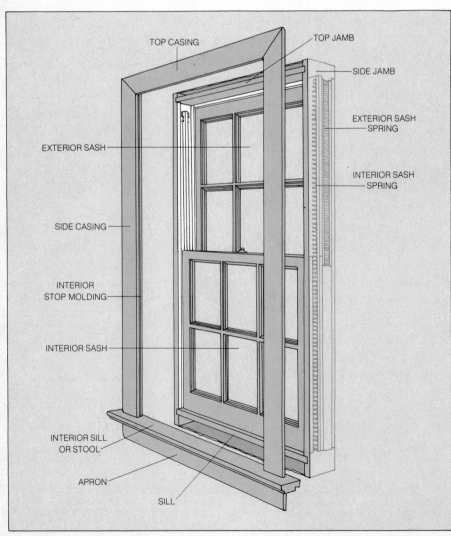

TOP CASING
TOP JAMB
SIDE JAMB
EXTERIOR SASH SPRING
EXTERIOR SASH
INTERIOR SASH SPRING
SIDE CASING
INTERIOR STOP MOLDING
INTERIOR SASH
INTERIOR SILL OR STOOL
APRON
SILL

Removing the Window

1 Removing the trim. Using a utility bar and hammer, pry off the casing from the front of the jamb at the top and sides of the window. Remove the strips of stop molding at the sides of the window and then the apron under the interior sill, or stool. Strike the underside of the stool with a small sledge to knock it up off the frame. Then pull out any nails protruding from the jamb.

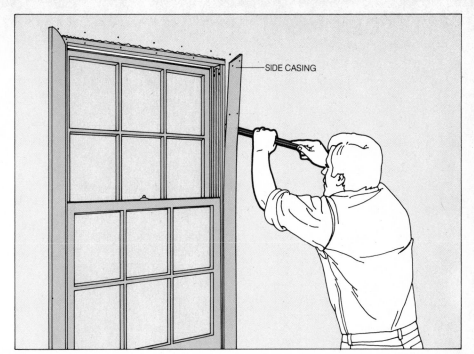

SIDE CASING

EXTERIOR SASH CHANNEL

INTERIOR SASH SPRING

PARTING STRIP

INTERIOR SASH CORD

PULLEY

EXTERIOR SASH WEIGHT

INTERIOR SASH WEIGHT

2 Taking out the sashes. Push both sashes down and twist the tops of the metal strips covering the springs for the interior sash (*above, left*). Pull off the interior strips, release the springs and lift the interior sash out of the window. Working outside the house, use the utility bar and hammer to pry off the top and side exterior casing and the exterior stops. Then twist the tops of the metal strips covering the springs for the exterior sash, pull off the strips and release the springs so you can take out the exterior sash. Remove the remaining metal strips from the sides and top of the jamb. For a double-hung window with cords (*above, right*), cut the front sash cords and lift the interior sash out of the frame. The sash weights will pull the cords behind the side jambs; weights and cords can be removed when you take off the jambs (*overleaf*). Pry off the parting strip that separates the sash channels, cut the remaining sash cords and lift out the exterior sash. Remove the exterior casing and stops.

3 **Pulling out the jamb.** With a handsaw, cut the top jamb and the sill in half. Then, with the aid of a utility bar, pry the top jamb and sill out of the opening. Pull the side jambs off the jack studs and remove all the nails that are still protruding from the rough frame.

Preparing the New Opening

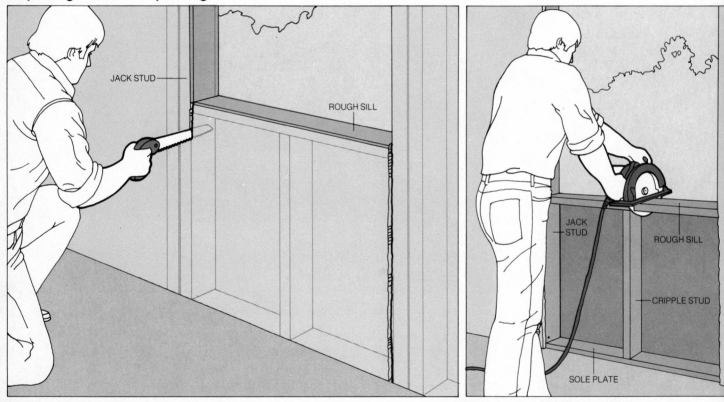

JACK STUD

ROUGH SILL

JACK STUD

ROUGH SILL

CRIPPLE STUD

SOLE PLATE

1 **Extending the interior opening.** Remove full sections of baseboard and molding from the working area (page 29, Step 4). With a keyhole saw, cut down the wall along one side edge of the window opening past the bottom of the rough sill—about 2 inches. Then, using the inner edge of the jack stud inside the wall as a guide for the saw blade, continue to cut down to the level of the sole plate.

Repeat the procedure on the other side of the window. Using the utility bar if necessary, pry off the wall-finishing material between the cuts. Now the inside of the wall will be exposed so you can see the existing framing.

2 **Taking out the rough sill.** Pull out any insulation material inside the wall. Then examine the sill of the rough opening to determine how it is attached to the jack studs. If the rough sill is toenailed between the studs (above), saw it in two near the middle and twist the ends off the studs. If the ends of the sill extend under the jack studs at the sides of the opening and separate jack studs support the bottom of the sill, saw out the sill flush with the inner edges of the studs and remove it. Twist the cripple stud under the sill off the sole plate at the bottom of the wall.

3 **Cutting away the siding.** Inside the house, measure from the bottom of the window opening to the sole plate, then add 1½ inches to allow for the depth of the plate. Outside, use a plumb line to snap lines down the siding to this distance from the bottom corners of the opening in the siding. Use a yardstick to draw a horizontal line between the ends of the vertical ones.

For wood, aluminum or stucco siding, set the blade of a circular saw—a carborundum blade for stucco—to the maximum depth of the siding. Cut along the lines, but avoid sawing into the sheathing; the border of sheathing left around the window opening will be continued for the door opening. Pry off siding between the cuts.

For brick siding, score the bricks along the drawn lines and remove the bricks inside the lines (*pages 92-93, Steps 1 and 3*).

4 **Extending the exterior opening.** Set the circular-saw blade to the depth of the sheathing. Then, using the inner edges of the jack studs to guide the blade, saw down the sheathing from the bottom corners of the window opening to the top edge of the remaining siding. Saw horizontally between the bottom ends of the cuts—along the top of the remaining siding. The sheathing will fall out of the opening. Using a handsaw, cut through the ends of the sole plate flush with the jack studs at either side of the opening. Pry the plate off the subflooring.

SHEATHING

JACK STUD

SIDING

SOLE PLATE

5 **Putting up flashing.** If there is no flashing above the opening, use metal shears to cut a strip of 6-inch aluminum flashing material long enough to cover the top casing of the door. Shape the flashing (*inset*) by tacking it to a 2-by-4, letting one long edge project ½ inch. Use gloved fingers or a block of wood to bend the projection down at a 90° angle against the side of the 2-by-4. Then untack the flashing, turn it over so you can make another bend in the opposite direction and retack it, this time letting the bent edge project 1½ inches or the depth of the top casing. Untack the flashing, and hold the bent section toward you. Then slip the 4-inch flat section up between the siding and sheathing at the top of the opening.

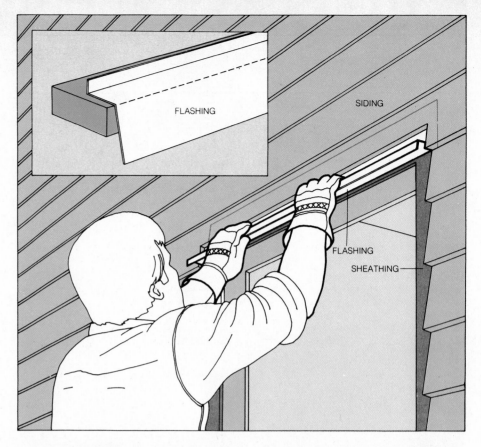

Fitting and Finishing an Exterior Door

1 **Setting the frame in the doorway.** If the door is hung from the frame, remove the pins from the hinges and take off the door. Then center the jamb in the opening and push it back so the outside trim lies flat against the sheathing and butts against the siding at the top and sides. Use a carpenter's level to determine which bottom corner of the sill is higher, then drive an eightpenny finishing nail into the side jamb 5 or 6 inches above the high corner. With your hand, push a wood wedge or shim under the opposite corner to level the sill. Nail that side jamb.

Push the frame backward and forward in the opening until it is plumb; if necessary, insert shims at the back of the top casing. Drive nails partway into the side jambs about a foot below the top corners, then hang the door on its hinges and follow the directions on page 43, Step 2 to shim the door from the inside. Pack strips of fiberglass insulating material around the top and side jambs of the door.

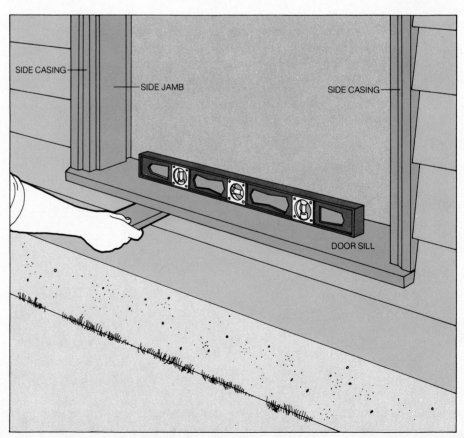

2 **Finishing the exterior.** Nail the top and side casings to the header and jack studs behind them, spacing the nails at 12-inch intervals. Drive in the nails in the side jambs and nail the exterior sill to the subflooring in two or three places. Countersink the nails and fill the holes with wood putty. Smooth the flashing across the top and down over the front of the top casing. Finally, caulk around the sides and bottom of the door.

3 **Starting the interior trim.** Inside the house, measure the inside width of the top jamb and add ¼ inch. Mark this distance on the side of the interior casing that will face the door, then make a 45° outward miter cut from each mark. Center the narrow side of the casing on the inner edge of the top jamb, ⅛ inch above the edge, with the ends extending ⅛ inch beyond the inner edges of the side jambs. Secure the casing first to the jamb, then to the header above the jamb with eightpenny finishing nails.

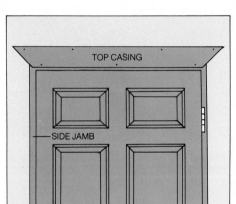

4 **Finishing the interior.** Square off one end of a casing strip, then butt that end against the floor and hold the strip over one side jamb to mark both the point where the strip meets the inner corner of the top casing and also the direction for your miter cut. Miter the casing and attach it—starting at the top—⅛ inch from the inner edge of the side jamb. Repeat the marking, cutting and nailing procedure to trim the other side jamb. Replace the molding and base shoe on either side of the opening. Set all the nails and fill the holes with wood putty. Finally, install the lockset, following the manufacturer's directions.

A Window or Door Where There Was None

No matter what kind of material covers a house—wood, aluminum, stucco or brick—its basic structure is probably frame; that is, it has walls of wood studs and plates. And with any frame house the techniques for making a new door or window opening are much the same. A section of the interior wall is removed, an opening is cut through the exterior cover, studs are taken out and a new frame is built for a prehung door or window. A more complex procedure (pages 95-97) is required in solid masonry houses—with brick or concrete structural walls—which are rare today.

Wood, aluminum and stucco are the easiest to cut through; you need only run a power saw around the edges of the opening, pry off the covering and remove a section of the framing. Brick veneer is treated separately on pages 92-94.

Planning the location of the opening can involve compromises. Inside the house you may want the new window or door to fit a certain decorating plan or a traffic pattern; outside, it may have to align with existing openings. If there are plumbing or electric lines at the location you have chosen, you must either move them or choose a new location.

Finally, you must align the inside and outside plans for your opening. The easiest method is to measure an equal distance, inside and out, from an existing window or door. If the wall does not have a door or window, drill a pilot hole through the wall with a long bit (a masonry bit for a brick veneer wall) and use the hole as a reference point.

Within the opening, you must install a frame. It resembles one for an interior partition, except that a stronger header supports the weight of the wall above. In place of a single 2-by-4 (page 35, Step 2),

two pieces of 2-by-6 or larger stock are nailed with a ½-inch plywood filler to form a stiff lumber sandwich; the size of the stock depends on the width of the header (chart, page 53).

If you want to make a wide opening—for a picture window or sliding patio doors—you can do so fairly simply provided the exterior is wood, aluminum or stucco and the wall does not support the structure above it. In such a nonbearing wall, which runs parallel to floor joists and roof rafters, the opening can be as wide as you please; in a bearing wall, which runs across joists and rafters, or in a brick veneer wall, an opening wider than 40 inches calls for professional guidance. So does any opening in an area containing a heavy steel or timber beam rather than conventional studs—here, shoring may be needed to support the house while new framing is installed.

Cutting a Neat Hole in Siding or Stucco

1 **Opening the interior.** After marking the rough location of the opening, remove full sections of baseboard and molding from the working area (page 29, Step 4). With a saber saw or a circular saw set to the depth of the wall covering, cut through the plaster or wallboard from floor to ceiling just inside the two studs to the left and right of the working area. Use a pry bar and your hands to rip away the wallboard or the plaster and lath inside the lines you have cut (you will need snips to cut away metal lath). Remove any insulation inside the wall.

2 Marking the outside of the opening. For a new door, use a pilot hole or an existing door or window to measure from, and mark the level of the subfloor on the outside. From the subfloor line, measure up and mark the height of the doorjamb, including trim, plus ⅛ inch for clearance. Connect the top and subfloor line, using a plumb line or a level to mark one side of the opening, then measure and mark the width of the door (between the outside edges of the casings)—plus ¼ inch for clearance. Outline the opening with a level.

For a window, you can set the top at any convenient height, though you may wish to match the level of existing windows. Measure the width as for a door. Measure the height of a wood window from the top of its casing to the bottom of its sill; measure a metal window on the trimmed wood box (*pages 100-101, Steps 1-3*). Add ¼ inch for clearances. Remove the exterior wall covering inside the marked perimeter with a circular saw (*page 85, Step 3*).

3 Cutting the sheathing. Measure the back of the top and side casing of the door or window (*inset*) and cut a hole in the sheathing that much smaller than the exterior opening. For a door, cut away the bottom of the sheathing all the way down to the bottom of the exterior opening. For a window, leave enough to fit behind the lip of the sill. This opening will be just large enough to slide the door or window jamb through.

4 **Preparing the interior.** Inside the house, saw through the middle of any studs in the wall opening. Use a pry bar to lever them away from the remaining plywood or fiberboard wall sheathing—try not to tear the sheathing near the edges of the opening—and pull them away from the top and sole plates; the temporary removal of these studs until the new framing can be installed will not endanger the wall.

Framing the Hole

1 **Erecting the frame.** Install outer studs and jack studs *(page 35, Step 1)* at the left and right of the sheathing opening with eightpenny nails. The jack studs should stand behind the sheathing that protrudes into the exterior opening, and the tops of the jack studs should be even with the top of the sheathing opening.

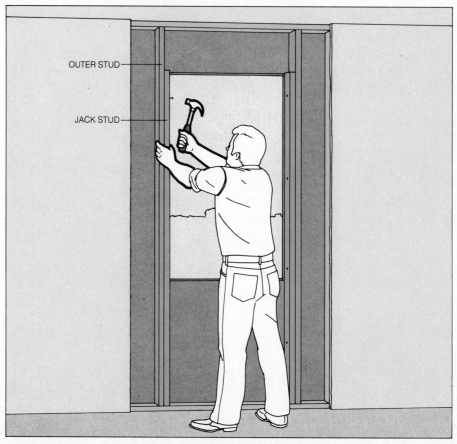

2 **Making the header.** Consult the chart *(page 53)* for the proper board size and cut two header boards to fit horizontally between the outer studs. The header *(inset)* must be as thick as the wall studs; to bring it to the correct thickness, insert ½-inch fillers between the header boards—scrap plywood will do—and nail the sandwich together with 16-penny nails. Set the header on edge on the jack studs and fasten it in place with two 16-penny nails driven through the outer studs into the header. Fit cripple studs between the header and top plate at each point where a regular stud was removed and toenail them in place with eightpenny nails.

HEADER

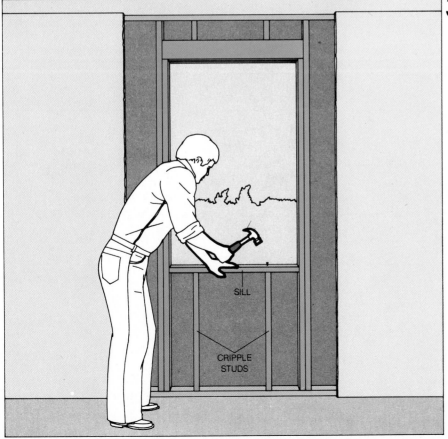

3 **Finishing the rough frame.** For a door, cut away the sole plate from between the insides of the jack studs. For a window, toenail a sill—a 2-by-4 on its side—between the jack studs just behind the bottom of the sheathing opening. Position cripples between the bottom of the sill and the sole plate at each point where a regular stud was removed. Drive 16-penny nails through the sill into the tops of the cripple studs and toenail the bottoms of the cripples to the sole plate with eightpenny nails.

SILL

CRIPPLE
STUDS

Breaking through Bricks

Cutting through a veneer of brick on a frame house for a new door or window involves more steps than cutting through wood, aluminum or stucco. A rigid lintel—a length of steel, L shaped in cross section, that you buy cut to length from a steel supplier—must be inserted to support the masonry above the new opening, and cutting the brick itself calls for strength and patience. First you must score the brick, using a circular saw and a carborundum blade so that the brick will break cleanly—a job that can take several hours. Removing the brick with a heavy hammer and a cold chisel also requires time and effort.

Though the job is difficult, it is perfectly safe. After you have made a hole, most of the bricks above stay in place, thanks to strong mortar joints, until the metal support can be installed. Even in old brick walls, only a few bricks above a new opening are likely to fall out, and they are easily restored. In badly deteriorated walls so many bricks may tumble out that an arch forms above the opening, but the compressive force of the remaining bricks will keep the arch intact (the stability of the bricks above an opening has led masons to refer to brick walls as "self-healing").

The opening you make in a brick wall can be high enough for any standard door size; its width is another matter. An opening wider than 40 inches will require professional guidance.

1 **Scoring the brickwork.** Mark the opening as described in Step 2, page 89. Wear goggles and a respirator. Retract the blade guard of a circular saw and work the saw into the wall along one of the side lines of the opening. Move the saw slowly; cutting too fast will burn out blades. Check the saw frequently for overheating and take a break whenever it gets hot.

2 **Cutting a lintel channel.** As you cut the lintel channel, bricks above may tumble out; wear a hard helmet as well as gloves and goggles for this job. Using a cold chisel and hammer, break up the mortar around the center brick in the course above your scored opening, then break that brick and remove the pieces. Repeat the process on the bricks to the left and right until there is a channel at least one half of a full brick beyond the opening on each side; the space provides shoulders for the lintel to rest upon.

3 **Extending the opening.** Remove the two courses beneath the lintel channel. To break off half bricks at the side of the opening, insert a broad-bladed mason's chisel, called a brickset, or a cold chisel into the score line with its bevel facing the inside of the opening and rap it sharply with a hammer. Save the bricks you remove; you will need some of them to rebrick the channel above the lintel.

4 **Setting the lintel.** Prepare about a quarter of a bucket of premixed brick mortar and trowel a coat ½ inch deep onto the top of each shoulder brick. Tip a precut lintel into the channel, with one leg of the L resting on the mortar and the other running up into the cavity behind the bricks. You may find that wall ties—short lengths of metal ribbon that join the brick to the wall studding—interfere with placement of the lintel; if so, cut the ties with a cold chisel.

LINTEL

MORTAR

SHOULDER

5 **Replacing brickwork.** Use a cold chisel to remove old mortar from the bricks you will reuse, and scrub them with a moistened wire brush; they should be damp but not wet. Prepare a bucket of premixed mortar and apply about a ⅜-inch coating to the top of the lintel. Apply mortar to the ends of a brick—if the brick above has remained in place, mortar the top as well—and lay it into the lintel at one end. Continue across the lintel, checking the top of the brick with a level; if necessary, remove bricks and make the mortar beneath them thicker or thinner to keep the course level and even with the remaining bricks at either side of the opening. Repeat the process above the lintel course until all the space over the lintel is rebricked; if you must cut bricks, follow the instructions in the box below.

6 **Completing the opening.** Working from the top to the bottom, and from the center to the sides, remove bricks to complete the opening. To remove the sheathing behind the bricks, see page 89, Step 3. To reframe the opening for a door or window, see pages 90-91.

How to Split a Brick

Wear goggles for this job to protect your eyes from flying chips. To cut brick in half, place a brickset or cold chisel across the brick and tap the chisel several times with a hammer to score a line, then place the brick on a bed of sand and strike the chisel with a sharp blow. The brick will separate into two pieces. To cut a brick lengthwise, secure it in a vise and cut through it with a circular saw fitted with a carborundum blade.

Techniques for Solid Masonry

Three types of solid masonry are likely to be encountered, and all can be opened for a new door or window, using many of the same techniques as for brick veneer *(pages 92-94)*.

The most common type is the single thickness of 8-inch concrete block or cinder block widely used for basement and garage walls. Block walls may also have a face veneer of a single course of brick over a course of 4-inch-thick block. And some old homes have solid walls consisting of two courses of brick. In both solid brick and brick-and-block construction, a ½-inch air space is often left between the courses. Score the opening the same way as for veneer, but do the back as well as the front; at least one pilot hole should be used to ensure that the front and back scoring registers exactly.

Rough-framing the opening is simpler in solid masonry than in a veneered house; a lintel of doubled-steel angle for brick, or precast concrete for block, supports the weight of the house. Steel lintels are available from steel suppliers; dealers in masonry materials can supply concrete lintels. A rough frame, made from 2-by-4s or 2-by-8s, serves as a nailing surface for the new door or window unit and as trim covering the ragged cores of broken-out block.

Rough-framing the opening. Cut a piece of 2-by-4 equal to the width of the opening for a header. If a window is to be installed, cut another piece the same length for a rough sill. Cut side pieces long enough to complete either the three-sided rough doorframe or four-sided window frame and fasten the frame together by driving 16-penny nails through the header (and sill for a window) into the ends of the side pieces. Set the frame in the opening flush with the interior face of the wall and drive eightpenny cut nails—heavy rectangular masonry nails—through the frame into the mortar joints between bricks.

Framing in Double Brick Walls

Installing a double lintel. Break out two courses of brick above the scored opening on both the inside and outside faces of the wall, using the techniques shown on page 93, Step 2. Mortar the shoulder bricks at either side of the opening on which the lintels are to rest. Place two steel lintels back to back and push them onto the mortared shoulders until their upright backs stand directly under the cavity between the faces. If the lintel increases the thickness of the wall so that bricks replaced on top of the lintel *(opposite, Step 5)* protrude beyond the face of the wall, cut their backs off using the brick-cutting techniques shown in the box at left. Break out the rest of the opening as shown on page 93 for a veneer wall.

Framing in Block Walls

Preparing the opening. Measure and score the opening inside and outside as you would for a solid brick wall *(page 92)*, but in a wall without a veneer, increase the size of the opening to allow for an outer frame: Add 1½ inches to the width of either a door or window opening; add ¾ inch to the height for a door, 1½ inches to the height for a window. In a veneered wall the outer frame is not needed. Break out a lintel channel *(page 93)*. If the shoulder blocks on which the lintel is to rest have been broken, break them out completely and replace them with solid-core concrete blocks. If they remain intact, tamp newspaper tightly to the bottom of the hollow cores. Fill the cores with mortar, which need not set before installing the lintel.

SHOULDER BLOCK

SHOULDER BLOCK

Setting the lintel. Order a precast reinforced lintel that is as thick and as tall as the blocks in your wall and as wide as the opening you have made for the channel. Mortar the shoulder blocks and—with a strong helper—lift the lintel into place. You may need to buy new blocks for repairing above the lintel; unlike bricks, cinder blocks are difficult to remove intact for reuse. In a brick-and-block wall, install a steel lintel in the brick veneer course, using the procedure described on pages 93-94, Steps 2-6.

Attaching nailers. In 8-inch-block walls that have core openings an inch or more deep, cut six 3-inch pieces of 1-by-4 or larger stock, and fasten them into the cores with cut nails, to fill the core space. Using these nailers to secure the outer framing, rather than nailing the framing directly to the block, avoids chipping the block. In a 4-inch-block wall (or if the cores in 8-inch block are not deep enough to hold the nailing blocks) you will have to secure the framing directly to the masonry with cut nails.

Outer framing for 8-inch block. From 1-by-8 stock cut a header (and sill if needed for a window) as wide as the opening. Since some will remain exposed, you may want to use a good grade of lumber. Cut two sidepieces long enough to complete the three-sided doorframe or four-sided window frame. Nail the header (and sill) to the sidepieces and slide the frame into the opening. Secure it with sixpenny nails into the nailing blocks or sixpenny cut nails into the scored masonry at the front and back of the opening. Repair any chipped blocks with mortar.

Completing the rough frame. Build a rough frame *(page 95)*, slide it into the outer frame so that it is flush with the inside of the opening, and nail it to the outer frame with sixpenny nails.

For a brick/block wall *(above, right)*, build the rough frame and anchor it directly to the opening in the block course with sixpenny cut nails.

Putting In a New Window

Factory-fabricated units make the fitting of a new window into a rough opening a straightforward carpentry job. The easiest to install are wood ones—the double-hung type is illustrated but other styles are available. They come fully assembled and glazed with exterior trim already attached, and are installed the same way regardless of style. All you need to do is tip the window into place, level and secure it and finish the interior trim.

Wood windows are made in two standard thicknesses for use with wood, aluminum or stucco-on-mesh siding: $4\frac{5}{8}$ inches thick to match wallboard interiors and $5\frac{3}{8}$ inches thick to match plaster ones. For use with masonry walls, the wood window is recessed until the inside edges are flush with the interior walls.

Where you need a metal unit for convenience or to blend with the existing windows, your best bet is a replacement window—so called because it is usually used to replace worn sashes in old wood jambs. Because these windows are only about 3 inches thick, however, you will need to build a boxlike frame of the same thickness as the wall to hold the unit in the rough opening. You also will have to add both exterior and interior wood stops and trim to the units. Replacement metal windows are widely available in sliding and double-hung styles; other styles may be hard to find.

When purchasing a window, metal or wood, be careful you do not buy a type—meant for new construction—that has nailing flanges, or fins, projecting from the jamb. These fins must be tucked between the exterior siding and sheathing. If you use such units for remodeling, you will need to remove siding all around the opening before you install the window and then replace it afterward.

1 Tipping in the window. With wood or aluminum siding or a stucco-on-mesh exterior, install flashing over the window opening, following the directions on page 86, Step 5. Set the window unit in the opening, pushing it up under the flashing. Shove the window back so the exterior casing fits firmly against the sheathing.

With a masonry exterior, recess the window to fit against the rough frame. The masonry will overhang the window so flashing is not necessary.

Windows with Wood Frames

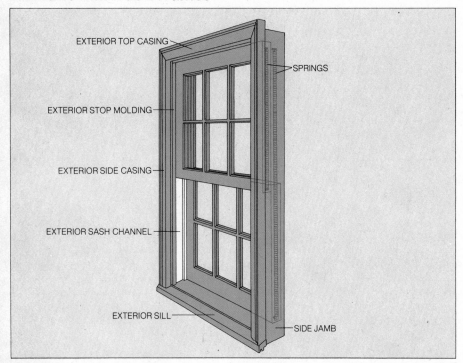

EXTERIOR TOP CASING

SPRINGS

EXTERIOR STOP MOLDING

EXTERIOR SIDE CASING

EXTERIOR SASH CHANNEL

EXTERIOR SILL

SIDE JAMB

SHEATHING

FLASHING

ROUGH SILL

Anatomy of a double-hung window. The upper, or exterior, sash of a double-hung window slides down and the lower, or interior, sash slides up in separate channels mounted on the side jambs. Springs concealed inside metal channels balance the weight of each sash so that it is easy to open and stays open in any position. Exterior, or blind, stops conceal the channels, shield the metal and help keep out drafts. Casing, or trim, attached to the header and jack studs of the rough opening, covers the outside edges of the top and side jambs. The exterior sill slopes outward to lead rain away from the bottom of the window; for wood, aluminum or stucco exteriors, the top edges of the casing are covered with protective flashing.

2 Adjusting the window. Measure how far the jamb of the window extends into the house. If the distance is less than the thickness of the wall-finishing material you plan to use, cut ¾-inch-wide wood strips of the additional thickness required to the length of the top and side jambs. Glue the strips to the interior edges of the jamb and secure them with eightpenny finishing nails (*right*). If the frame juts into the room too far, take the window out of the opening and nail wood fillers of the same width as the exterior casing around the top and sides of the exterior edges of the jamb to extend the whole unit farther out from the wall of the house.

JAMB
EXTENSIONS

3 Leveling and plumbing the window. Working outside the house, center the window between the jack studs. Lift the unit until the top jamb butts against the bottom of the header. Use a carpenter's level to determine which side of the window is lower. Nail the lower top corner to the header with an eightpenny finishing nail. Lower the other top corner until the window is level and nail that corner in place.

Inside the house, check the level, then wedge shims between the bottom of the window and the rough sill. Nail through the shims into the sill. Plumb the window from front to back—inserting at least two shims on each side—and insulate around it with strips of fiberglass material. Finally, secure and caulk the exterior casing, following the directions on page 87, Step 2.

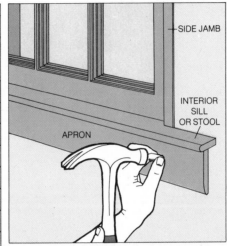

SIDE JAMB

INTERIOR
SILL
OR STOOL

APRON

4 Attaching the interior sill. Finish the interior wall, following the procedures on pages 36-41 and butting the material against the window jamb. Cut the interior sill, or stool, long enough to cover the front of the frame and extend on each side at least to the width of the decorative casing you plan to use over the jambs. Notch the back of the sill at both ends so the center section will fit between the side jambs and, if desired, use a wood file and sandpaper to shape the ends. Then set the sill in place and anchor it to the bottom of the window frame with finishing nails. Cut casing or apron molding 1 inch shorter than the sill to make an apron for covering the joint under the sill, shaping the ends if desired. Nail the apron to the studs below the window.

INTERIOR STOP MOLDING

INTERIOR SIDE CASING

5 Finishing the interior trim. Bend the projecting strips of sash channel flat against the interior sash and measure from the strips to the front of the side jambs—usually ½ inch. Cut two strips of interior stop molding of this thickness to fit inside the jamb from the top to the sill. Set the strips flush with the front of the side jambs and nail them in place.

To prepare decorative casing that will cover the front of the stops as well as the side and top jambs of the window, measure the sides and top from the inner corners of the stops. Then follow the directions on page 87, Steps 3 and 4 to miter, cut and attach the casing. Countersink all interior trim nails and fill the holes with plastic wood. Finally, finish the window and attach the window lock and lift.

Windows with Metal Frames

Anatomy of a metal replacement window. The sashes of a sliding (*right*) or double-hung metal window run in separate preformed channels mounted inside the jamb of the unit. The sashes are weather-stripped inside and out and the side jambs are weather-stripped around the outer edges of the sash channels. Vents on the exterior sill of the unit prevent moisture from accumulating inside the bottom of the frame. A separate top piece called a header expander provides about half an inch of vertical adjustment to fit the unit snugly into an existing frame or a specially constructed box frame (*below*).

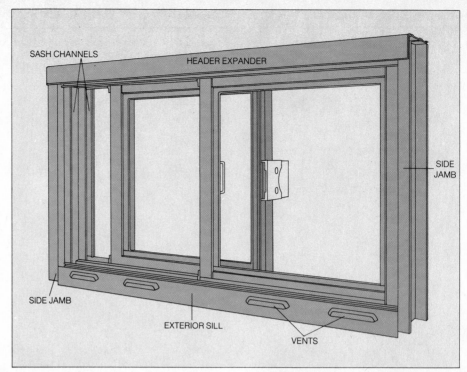

SASH CHANNELS

HEADER EXPANDER

SIDE JAMB

SIDE JAMB

EXTERIOR SILL

VENTS

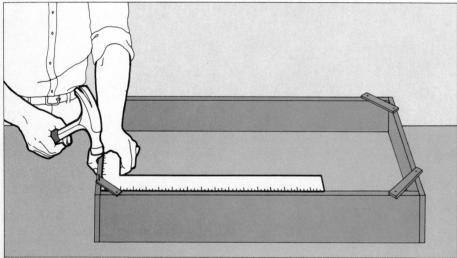

1 Making the box frame. Using 1-inch lumber wide enough to extend from the exterior of the sheathing to the interior of the finished wall, cut two side pieces 2 inches longer than the height of the window, then top and bottom pieces ½ inch longer than the width of the window. Assemble the four pieces of the box, as shown, with eightpenny box nails. With a carpenter's square, adjust one corner at a time into a perfect 90° angle and add a brace of scrap wood on the interior side of the box.

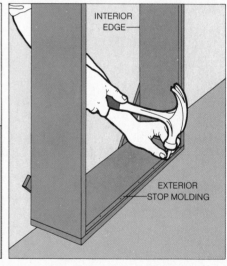

INTERIOR EDGE

EXTERIOR STOP MOLDING

2 Adding exterior stops. Measure the thickness of the window unit and add the thickness of the interior window stop molding you plan to use. Draw lines at this distance from the interior edge of the box inside both sides and across the top. Measure and cut exterior stop molding to fit inside the box from the bottom to the top on each side, and across the top between them. Align the inner edges of the stop molding strips with the lines and secure the stops in place with eightpenny finishing nails.

3 **Trimming and installing the box.** Measure the inside width and height of the box and deduct ¼ inch from each figure. Working along the edge of the exterior casing that you want to face the window, mark the length of one side casing and make 45° outward miter cuts from the marks. Repeat this process to cut a second side casing as well as casing strips for the top and bottom of the window. Set one casing strip at a time on the exterior edge of the box, positioning the narrow side of the strip ⅛ inch from the inside of the box. Attach the strip to the box with eightpenny finishing nails. Install the trimmed box in the rough opening, then level and plumb it *(page 99, Step 3)*. Nail the top of the box to the header from inside the house and remove the braces; secure and caulk the exterior casing.

4 **Putting in the window.** Run a bead of exterior caulking compound along the inner edges of the side and top exterior stops. Then place the header expander on top of the window frame and slide the unit into the box, butting it up against the exterior stops.

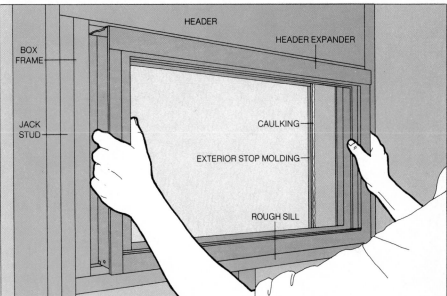

HEADER

HEADER EXPANDER

BOX FRAME

JACK STUD

CAULKING

EXTERIOR STOP MOLDING

ROUGH SILL

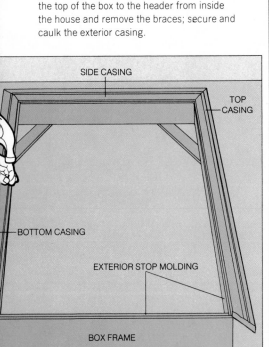

SIDE CASING

TOP CASING

BOTTOM CASING

EXTERIOR STOP MOLDING

BOX FRAME

SIDE CASING

5 **Securing the window.** For a sliding window, drive the screws that come with the unit partway into both the top and bottom holes on the side jambs. Insert the sashes and try moving them back and forth. If the sashes move easily, tighten the screws. Otherwise, insert shims between the metal frame and the box to level the window before tightening the screws.

For a double-hung window, drive screws only into the top holes. Then insert the sashes and use the special alignment screws located in the center of the side jambs to correct the sash movement. When the sashes slide easily, insert the bottom screws and tighten the top ones.

6 **Finishing the interior.** Push the expander header up tight against the top of the box with the blade of a screwdriver. Drill a ⅛-inch hole about ¼ inch inside each top corner of the expander, then secure the expander with the screws provided with the unit. Finish the interior wall, *(pages 36-41)*, butting the material against the box frame. If you want to trim the frame to match other windows in the room, follow the directions on page 99, Steps 4 and 5 to add a sill, apron, side stops and decorative casing. Alternatively you can leave the edges of the box visible and cut interior stop molding to fit inside it along the sides from the bottom to the top, and across the top and bottom between the side stops. Beginning with the sides, set one strip at a time inside the box flush with the interior edge and secure it with finishing nails.

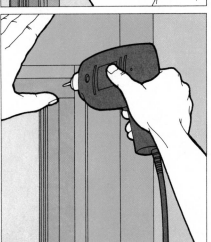

A Comfortable Climate in a New Living Space

To be livable, a new room must be heated and insulated—and insulation comes first. Insulating materials are installed before wallboards or ceilings go up; electric or gas heaters (pages 104-105) may be installed in finished or unfinished rooms.

The insulation not only makes new living spaces feel comfortable, but also cuts heating and cooling costs. It comes in two basic forms for home installation on unfinished walls or ceilings: blankets or batts, consisting of fibrous sheets of insulating material attached to paper or metal foil, and rigid insulating boards or panels.

Blankets come in long rolls; batts in precut rectangles, usually 4 or 8 feet long. Both come in widths that fit between joists or studs, and in varying thicknesses up to 7½ inches. It is a good rule to install the thickest insulation you can fit between joists and studs.

Both blankets and batts can be purchased with a vapor barrier of chemically treated or foil-lined paper that prevents the moisture-laden air of a heated room from penetrating the insulation material. Blankets and batts for use between studs and rafters usually come with stapling

flanges at each side to make installation easier. Friction-fit batts, usually used between floor joists (opposite, top right), do not have flanges.

Rigid polystyrene insulation panels are often used on the masonry walls of basements. They are relatively expensive but they are especially efficient insulators, are easily installed between furring strips and do not require vapor barriers. In the example shown below, the insulation value can be doubled by using 2-by-2s for furring strips and installing double thicknesses of paneling.

Insulating a masonry wall. Measure across the top and bottom of the wall and cut two 1-by-2 wood strips to this length. At each end of one of the strips mark off a block 1½ inches wide across the flat side of the strip. Make similar marks at 16-inch intervals measured from the center of one mark to the center of the next; the last two marks may be closer. Lay the two strips side by side and copy the markings from one to the other (page 28, Step 1). Nail one strip across the top of the wall, the other across the bottom, using sixpenny cut nails at 24-inch intervals. Measure the distance between the two strips and nail 1-by-2s of this length from the

top marks to the bottom marks, using four sixpenny cut nails per strip. Cut additional 1-by-2s to make frames around windows or doors. A precise fit is not essential in this stage of the job. To complete the pattern of furring strips, cut 1-by-2s into 14½-inch lengths and nail them horizontally between the vertical strips, exactly 4 feet above the bottom strip. If necessary, use a carpenter's level and a plumb bob to check the vertical and horizontal alignment of the strips.

Fit insulation panels, each 4 feet by 14½ inches, between the strips at the bottom of the wall; to secure the panels in place, apply mas-

tic adhesive evenly around the edges and in an X pattern across the center. Cut additional panels to fit snugly between the horizontal strips and the ceiling and fit these panel sections in place similarly, butting them firmly with the horizontal strips to form a tight joint. Save the trimmed panel scraps for piecing around windows or doors.

Insulating an attic floor. To prevent heat loss through an attic floor outside a new room in the attic, use blankets or batts between the floor joists beyond the knee walls. Wearing gloves and goggles, trim the blankets or batts to run from the wall to a point just short of the floor vents in the eaves. These vents must be kept clear to provide ventilation in the attic. Then lay the fitted blankets or batts between the joists with the vapor-barrier side down.

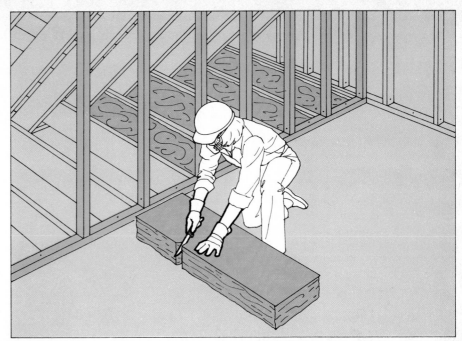

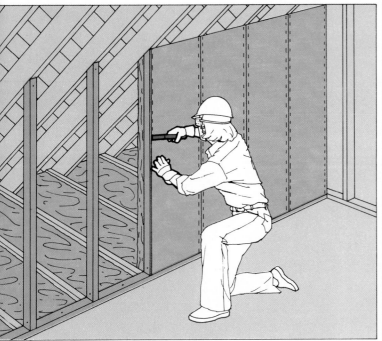

Insulating between studs and joists. To insulate walls and ceilings, use blankets with stapling flanges on the sides. Fit insulation between studs or ceiling joists, vapor-barrier side facing you. Staple flanges to flanking studs or joists at 6-inch intervals. In attic knee walls, fit insulation so it meets the insulation placed between joists (*above*) so warm air cannot escape. Similarly, make sure insulation fits tightly at the knee-wall/stud-rafter joint. For attic ceilings, cut blankets to rafter-to-rafter measurements with about an inch extra on each end. Notch each end to fit the collar beam-rafter junction; staple at 6-inch intervals to the collar beam.

Insulating between rafters. Select a blanket or batt thickness that allows at least ½ inch of space between the insulation and the roof sheathing, so that air can circulate freely from eave and ridgepole vents. Starting where the rafter is intersected by the ceiling collar beam, staple the blankets, vapor-barrier side facing you, firmly to rafters at 6-inch intervals. Allow a slight overhang at the bottom to fit behind the knee-wall insulation. Use plastic or duct tape to cover the seams where the rafter insulation meets the ceiling and knee-wall insulation.

An Independent Source of Heat

The self-contained electric or gas heating units called space heaters, which operate independently of the main house furnace, offer a convenient way to heat a new living area. Electric baseboard heaters are especially easy to install. They do not require additions to existing ductwork and they make no demands upon a house heating plant that may already be taxed to its capacity.

When buying any heating unit, give the supplier the measurements of your new room and its windows and, if possible, the amount of insulation and the average hours of daily winter sunlight. From this data, the dealer can tell approximately how much heat the room needs, measured in British thermal units per hour. (A BTU is the amount of heat needed to raise the temperature of one pound of water one degree.)

An electric baseboard unit delivers about 3.4 BTUs per hour for each watt of power it consumes. As a rule of thumb, plan to install about 10 watts of electric heat for every square foot of floor area; in a small bedroom, for example, you might need 1,200 watts, or over 4,000 BTUs per hour. Baseboard heaters for ordinary household 120-volt circuits come in units drawing up to 1,500 watts of power. For maximum comfort they should be installed on exterior walls.

Some electric heaters come with plugs, but most are meant to be connected directly to a power-supply cable. A plug-in heater may be adequate if your heating season is short or your new room gets infrequent winter use, but for most installations a permanent connection is preferable. It eliminates all exposed wiring—there is no cord for humans to trip over or pets to bite at—and makes a foolproof connection to an appliance that draws a large amount of current.

Ideally, a baseboard unit should be powered by its own circuit. If this is not practical, install a unit on a lightly used circuit; if you use more than one unit, connect them to different circuits. If there is any question about the adequacy of your wiring, you may need an electrician's help to analyze its capacity and install additional circuits for the new load.

1 Installing a baseboard heater. Lay the unit on the floor next to its planned location, remove the base shoe and the baseboard at that location, and mark locations for mounting clips or screws. In one common system (*below*) clips are screwed to the wall fit into slots in the heater back.

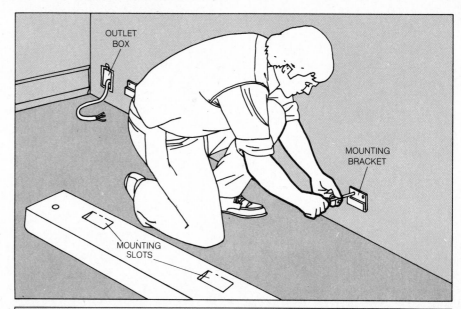

OUTLET BOX

MOUNTING BRACKET

MOUNTING SLOTS

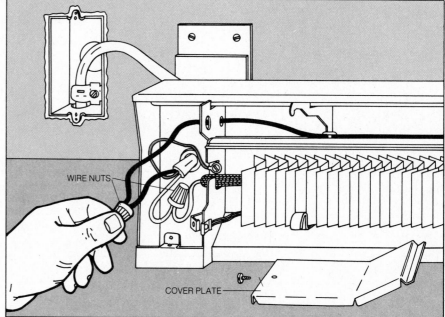

WIRE NUTS

COVER PLATE

2 Making a permanent connection. Wires for permanent installations are located in a wiring box at one end of the heater. Unscrew the front cover of this box and remove a knockout from its back, bottom or end. Turn off the current to the power-supply cable by removing the fuse or switching off the circuit breaker. Fit the knockout hole with a cable clamp and install the cable from an outlet box directly behind the location you have chosen for the heater. If this placement is inconvenient, your local electrical code may permit you to run the cable directly into the heater's wiring box through a hole in the wallboard; check the code to be sure. Strip about ¾ inch of insulation from the black and white cable wires and, using wire nuts, connect these wires to the black and white wires of the heater. Connect the bare ground wire of the cable to the green screw terminal in the wiring box. Replace the cover of the box and complete the installation by slipping the heater onto the wall clips. If the unit has a wire for a separate thermostat, be sure that this wire is free.

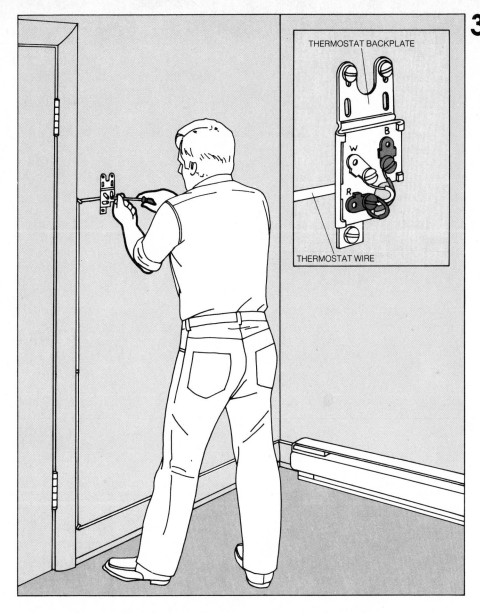

THERMOSTAT BACKPLATE

THERMOSTAT WIRE

3 **Mounting a thermostat.** A heater intended for use with a separate thermostat is usually equipped with one and includes enough wire to install it. The manufacturer or distributor will connect this wire at the heater, but you must make the connections at the thermostat. Locate the thermostat at a spot that will not be affected by direct sunlight, drafts or the heater itself; if possible, place it near a door so that the doorframe will partially conceal the wiring.

From the heater, run the thermostat wires along baseboards, doorframe and walls to the thermostat location, and staple them in place. If you need more wire, buy three-strand thermostat wire; do not use bell wire. Attach the thermostat backplate to the wall, then connect the color-coded thermostat wires to the backplate terminals marked R for red, B for blue and W for white. Screw the thermostat and its cover to the backplate.

A Plug for Portability

GROUNDING SCREW

GREEN TERMINAL

Installing the receptacle. Plug-in heaters come equipped with several feet of three-wire power cord; if the cord is too short to reach the nearest outlet box replace it with a longer heavy-duty cord containing No. 14-gauge wire. Then, after disconnecting the current in the circuit that will serve the heater, install a three-hole receptacle in an outlet box already fitted with a power cable (*page 31*). Connect the black wire of the outlet box cable to a brass screw terminal on the receptacle and the white wire to a silver terminal; using a wire nut and two short jumper wires, connect the bare cable wire to the green screw terminal of the receptacle and to a grounding screw in the back of the box. Finally, fasten the receptacle to the outlet box and screw a cover plate over the entire assembly.

Heating with Gas

In most localities gas is a cheaper source of heat than electricity, especially for large rooms—gas heaters range in output from a few thousand to 90,000 BTUs per hour. In some areas, local regulations may permit you to connect the heater to your gas supply yourself, subject to an inspector's approval, but it is a job best left to a professional. Running a gas supply line to the heater requires experience in connecting and testing steel pipes—a less-than-perfect installation is a serious hazard. However, you can save money by installing the unit in the wall yourself; if possible, do it before putting up wallboard. Instructions for installation come with most models.

Some wall heaters are designed to sit on the floor next to a wall, some to be attached to a wall, and others to be recessed into a wall, fitting between two adjacent studs. Still others fit under floor grates, but this type is banned in some areas; the grates on certain models can get very hot and may be dangerous.

Expanding a House by Converting a Garage

Converting a garage into potential new living space involves replacing the car-entry door with a permanent wall and finishing the new wall's exterior to match or contrast with the finish of the rest of the garage and the house.

An old-fashioned, outward-opening garage door need only be taken off its hinges. You may prefer to entrust to a contractor the more complex task of removing a heavy, spring-powered section-al door, but as the diagrams show, it is possible to do it yourself.

Framing out the opening demands only the simple carpentry described on pages 28-29. Residential building codes usually require that a converted garage admit natural light through a window and door space roughly equal to one tenth of its floor area, and that at least half of this area must provide a ventilation opening. The easiest place to install a door or a pair of double-hung windows (pages 98-99) is in the new wall.

Finishing the new wall's outer face in-volves attaching siding that either match-es or complements the existing siding. An easy solution is to apply plywood siding (page 111) that contrasts with existing siding. Matching wood siding of shingles, vertical or horizontal boards (page 112), or panel plywood is more difficult but can produce an almost undetectable blend of old and new siding. Brick veneer is harder both to install and to match with existing masonry, and matching stucco is best left to a professional.

To align new siding with existing siding that overlaps the concrete floor of the garage, you may need to break up and remove the driveway apron. If you mere-ly wish to mask the effect of a driveway halting abruptly at the base of a wall, you can level the apron with concrete and build a planter across the new surface.

Releasing a Torsion Spring

1 Loosening the setscrews. If the weight of your sectional garage door is countered by a wind-up spring over the opening, lower the door to get at the spring. Take great care in unwinding the spring, which is at maximum tension with the door down. For this purpose use two strong metal winding rods—both at least 18 inches long and made of cold-rolled steel. Insert one rod in one of the holes in the winding cone. It should fit snugly. Keeping a firm grip on the rod to restrain the cone, loosen the cone's setscrews.

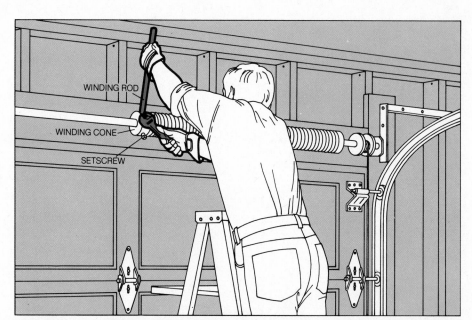

2 Unwinding the spring. Slowly release the spring, alternating the rods in the cone holes as the cone turns. Grip the rods near their ends to exert the fullest possible leverage on the spring. When the spring has unwound and the wire cable connecting it to the door is slack, unfasten the cable from the door.

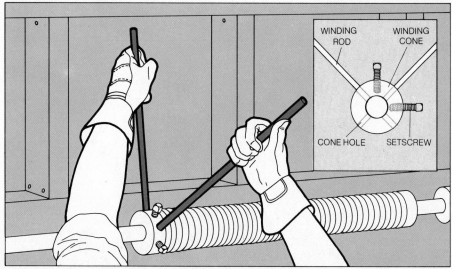

Unhooking extension springs. If the door has an extension spring on each side, raise the door to decrease spring tension. Brace the door open with two 2-by-4s. Carefully remove the S hook that anchors one end of one of the wire cables at a point near the entrance. Let this cable pass through the pulley at the end of the spring, then detach the other end of the cable from the door. Similarly remove the other cable, then remove the braces and lower the door.

Dismantling the door. Dismantle any sectional garage door from the top down. Remove the hinges and fixtures from the top section, then the section itself. Similarly remove each succeeding section. Remove a torsion shaft by unbolting it from the framing above the opening. Begin track removal at the rear of the garage. Unbolt the horizontal tracks from their supports, then unscrew the vertical tracks from the doorjamb.

Starting the Wall

1 **Uncovering header and studs.** Remove the jambs and all trim from around the door. Leave in place the two header beams across the top of the entrance. They support the wall above the opening and distribute its weight to the 2-by-4 studs on the sides of the opening to which you will attach the new wall frame.

2 **Placing the sole plate.** Measure and cut a length of lumber treated with wood preservative to fit between and align exactly with the existing sole plates on each side of the opening. It must be the same size in cross section as the two existing plates. Test the resistance of the concrete slab by trying to drive an eightpenny masonry nail through a scrap of lumber and into the slab. If the slab resists nailing, plan to use a low velocity stud driver to attach the new sole plate, or bolt it to the slab. To prepare for bolting, drill holes for ½-inch or ⅜-inch lag bolts at 24-inch intervals in the new sole plate. Set the plate in place, mark positions for corresponding holes on the slab and remove the plate. Then drill holes in the slab an inch deep and ⅛ inch wider than the holes in the sole plate, and insert lead shields.

3 Attaching the sole plate. Lay an 8-inch strip of copper or aluminum termite shield—or aluminum flashing if termite shield is unavailable—across the opening with its outer 2 inches overhanging the edge of the slab. Lay the new sole plate in place, taking care not to tear the termite shield, and toenail it to the existing plates. Fold the termite shield down over the slab edge at a 30° angle with the edge. Attach the sole plate to the slab with eightpenny masonry nails at 2-foot intervals, or by screwing lag bolts into holes that were prepared previously.

SOLE PLATE

TERMITE SHIELD

4 Constructing the wall frame. Measure all four sides of the opening. Construct a wall frame as shown on pages 28-31. Rough-frame any window or door openings in the frame as illustrated on pages 90-91. To frame an opening for two double-hung windows, halve the opening by nailing a divisional mullion stud between the top plate and the rough sill of the window frame. Raise and fasten the wall frame in place as directed on pages 28-31, then toenail the center stud into place on the sill. If the window casings will require additional backing, add another divisional stud or shim as needed. If narrow casings do not butt over the divisional stud, cover the stud with a strip of trim. You may wish to buy a preassembled two-window unit, in which case you will not need the center stud.

Finishing the Wall

To finish off the space underneath the windows of a newly installed wall, most people prefer to make it match the exterior of the rest of the house. Matching aluminum siding *(page 118)* is generally fairly easy if it is made of standard-sized materials. Masonry presents difficulties—stucco calls for professional skills, and new bricks, even if identical to the ones originally used in constructing the house, will look different until they have weathered for many years. In such cases, the best solution is to avoid any attempt at a match; select a contrasting finish such as the one illustrated *(opposite)*.

The first step in matching wood siding—clapboard, shingle, shiplap or vertical boards—is to rip off some of the existing material. You will then have a sample to take to the lumberyard so that you can be sure of getting an identical match. You can also measure the thickness of the sheathing underneath and match its size. And you will be able to see how the old siding was nailed on so that you can do the same with the new.

All siding must be applied over sheathing. For shingles and vertical boards, the sheathing must provide a nailing surface—use C-D exterior sheathing plywood and nail over it strips of 15-pound felt paper, overlapping the edges. For horizontal siding such as the clapboard described below, you can use the lighter, less-expensive sheathing that is made of asphalt-impregnated fibers, this sheathing requires no paper covering.

Installing Horizontal Siding

1 Clearing the way. At each side of the newly framed and sheathed wall, pry off existing siding back to the first joint of each strip. If the nearest joint is far removed from the opening, cut a new joint with a saber saw. The staggered border of old siding on each side will let you interleave new siding with old for a uniform exterior.

Attaching sheathing. Mark the positions of the studs on the edge of the slab as a guide for nailing sheathing and siding. Fasten the sheathing with sixpenny box nails at 6-inch intervals on edges and 12 inches on intermediate studs.

Between joints leave an expansion space of 1/16 inch; in highly humid climates double that space. Where necessary, provide horizontal nailing blocking between studs. Install window units as shown on pages 98-99.

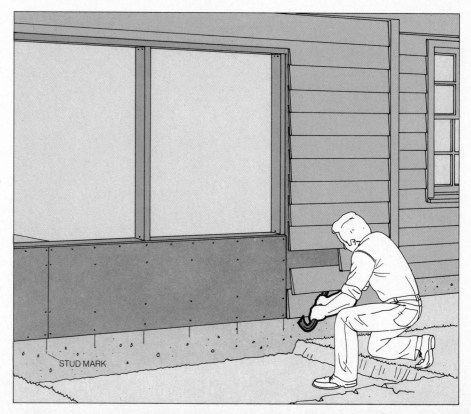

STUD MARK

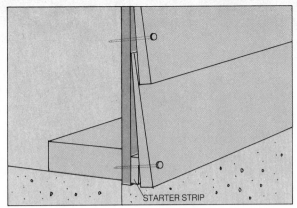

STARTER STRIP

2 **Adding siding.** Nail on the new siding from the bottom up, aligning each strip with the old siding on either side of it. If the bottom course of original siding is nailed over a starter strip, begin this application with a similar strip. Use weather-resistant (aluminum or galvanized) siding nails—sixpenny for siding ½ inch thick, eightpenny for ¾ inch. In bevel siding (left), drive one nail at each stud crossing, near the bottom edge of the board but above the board below, to allow the pieces to expand and contract individually. Shiplap is fastened with nails driven into its face 1 inch from each edge at each stud crossing.

Applying Contrasting Siding

1 **Attaching plywood panels.** If the existing exterior is difficult to match, apply a contrasting finish of exterior-grade plywood ⅝ inch thick. Cut the plywood to fit the opening in such a way that the grain of each piece runs in the same direction and the edges fall along the centers of studs. Caulk the edges, then set it with the edges 1⁄16 inch apart to allow for expansion. Drive eightpenny siding nails every 16 inches along the edges of each panel and at 12-inch intervals on intermediate studs, leaving a space of 1⁄16 inch at joints for expansion.

2 **Trimming the inset.** Caulk along the side edges of the plywood, then attach lengths of 1-by-2 with sixpenny siding nails.

A Creative Sense of Space

Space is as much an architectural resource as bricks or boards, but it is far more malleable—and sometimes it is free. Every dwelling, every room has space waiting to be used. Using it imaginatively can make a room more inviting, more comfortable or more useful.

If you open your mind before opening your toolbox, you may not need to get out the tools at all, for often it is possible to rethink an existing room rather than undertake a carpentry project. In many cases, rooms can be expanded by visual trickery alone. Mirrors, of course, offer an obvious way to double the impression of space in a room, and you do not need to live on the scale of Louis XIV to employ the dodge his architects used in the famous Hall of Mirrors in the palace at Versailles—its long line of mirrors faces a row of windows in the opposite wall, further increasing the expansion by reflecting the landscape outside.

There are subtler ways to stretch a limited space—light-colored walls and ceiling, and small-scale furniture sparingly arranged, make any room seem bigger. Elimination of clutter and barriers to vision always helps, for people need eye room as well as elbowroom. If you call attention to space that is visible even if not physically accessible—opening up odd corners such as alcoves under the eaves of an attic room—you can create an engaging sense of sprawl.

This same principle applies when you decide to take down a wall. Canny restraint—simply piercing or partially removing the wall—can often accomplish more for the final result than a bulldozing, straight-down-the-middle approach. A peek is often more enticing than total disclosure. In the view at right, the partial glimpses of rooms beyond rooms stretch the imagination and create an impression of reserves of space.

You can also make existing space do double duty. By building in rather than building on you can increase a room's utility without seriously interrupting the flow of space. You can build a loft into a corner of a high-ceilinged room in such a way that you gain a whole new level of living while the space beneath the loft remains as useful as ever. A compact office can be cunningly constructed within an existing room so as to provide a private, sheltered nook without diminishing—possibly even enhancing—the total effect of the room.

Such multiple use of space has been exploited by architects in the "open-plan" design used to make up for the small sizes of rooms in many modern homes. You can take advantage of the idea by removing partitions to combine two or more rooms with compatible functions. If you merge a kitchen, dining area and living room into one continuous whole you add not only a feeling of spaciousness but often extra utility. Opening the kitchen to the living-dining area allows the cook to join in conversations with family and guests, an arrangement that may improve both social occasions and the disposition of the cook.

Expanding the view. A combination of ingenious devices gives a spacious look to this long, narrow living-dining area in a Long Island weekend house. Low modular furniture and a cutout kitchen wall allow a partial view of rooms beyond, suggesting yet more available space. A long glass wall opens the room to the outside world, adding an impression of width, while the mobile hung from the ceiling directs attention to the already ample headroom and leads the eye up to the loft bedroom above the kitchen.

A

An Extra Dimension with Optical Illusions

Enlarging a room by deception is a time-tried device. Without removing a wall or raising a ceiling you can increase the sense of space in a cramped hallway or a confining living room simply by giving the eye room to roam. A mirrored wall adds the enticing illusion of another room. A glass-topped table seems to occupy less space than one that blocks a line of sight. Pale walls that reflect light close you in less than dark walls that soak up light. Large graphics or landscapes with strong and deep perspective can also add illusory depth to a room.

A trick with mirrors. A wide floor-to-ceiling mirror reflecting the small hallway of a London house (*left*) creates the illusion of room to spare. A transparent dining table—glass-topped, with clear plastic supports—enhances the effect by revealing additional floor space.

A trick with perspective. This giant diptych grabs the eye, drawing it insistently into the illusory depths of perspective. Low, muted furniture and bare walls help the dominant graphics to divert attention from the shallow space.

A trick with color. Light from outside is reflected by the cool white ceiling, floor and walls of this room in Sardinia. The shimmer of light on all these surfaces blurs the hard edges of reality and makes the walls and ceiling seem to recede.

Building New Uses into Old Rooms

Every home contains a few cubic feet that can be redefined, with the aid of imagination and elementary carpentry, by erecting structures that do not alter the building's basic framework. Building-in is a technique particularly attractive to apartment dwellers who do not have the option of knocking down walls or building on rooms.

Rooms may be divided vertically with handsome partitions that take the place of walls but open and close like doors. A room can also be sliced up horizontally by adding levels to be used for anything from sleeping to storage. Or a portion of a room can be turned into a sheltered corner to provide adolescents or adults who work at home with a comforting sense of privacy.

An oval office. A freestanding plaster wall in the bedroom of a Manhattan apartment creates an office with a rear entrance, slit window and a ceiling that supports lights and potted plants.

A bedroom on stilts. A platform tucked in under a high ceiling doubles the use of a room in a London flat. A sheet of particle board supported on slender but sturdy scaffolding of ordinary steel pipe creates a sleeping loft without obstructing the dining area below.

Two rooms from one. Stainless-steel panels cut a large Manhattan apartment room into two intimate living areas. The two middle panels, hung by steel rings from tracks in the ceiling, slide aside to make room for a party.

Multilevel living. Waist-high dividers define various multilevel living areas without interrupting the expansive sweep of this converted Manhattan factory loft. The kitchen-dining section overlooks the large open living room where a bank of storage cabinets covered with gray carpet ranges along the wall and a hexagonal conversation area rises in the far corner.

Borrowing and Revealing Space

You can increase the size of almost any room by borrowing from an adjoining room or by uncovering hidden space within the room itself. One way to enlarge a room is to combine two rooms by taking out the wall between them, but you can also add a feeling of space by merely piercing a wall. Windows in interior walls lure sight into adjoining rooms. Opening a ceiling gives a room instant uplift. And in an attic room, a dormer or skylight provides not only light and air but extra headroom.

Space also lurks in less expected places. Lowering a mantelpiece increases a room's apparent height. Opening a stairwell adds to the area around the stairs. And even a room large enough for the activities it must contain gains by expanding into quirkish corners.

Using every inch. An angular alcove under the eaves adds width to a renovated attic in an Italian condominium. The mirror effect of glossy white paint on walls and ceiling further increases the room's apparent size.

F

Inspirational space. Uncluttered walls speed the eye toward the lofty open ceiling of the living room in this Florida house. At the far end, windows, a doorway and a balcony intensify the sense of spaciousness by providing glimpses of other rooms and of the outdoors.

Instead of a hall. What was formerly a hall in this Manhattan duplex apartment has been merged with an adjoining room by removing most of the wall between them. To make maximum use of the nook enclosed by a remainder of the wall, a sofa was built into the space.

Showing off space. Vertical space becomes not only a virtue but the dominant theme of this three-story room created in a converted loft. Low furniture and giant art works emphasize the soaring height of the stark white walls. The mirror surface of the coffee table below and of the stainless-steel cabinets suspended from the ceiling of the balcony kitchen above contribute the illusion of still more space extending up past the ceiling and down through the floor.

The Remarkable 2-by-4

The mighty 2-by-4 is a major basic building block of house construction—and of remodeling. Used vertically for studs, horizontally for plates and fire stops, it makes up most of the walls in American houses, whether they are frame or masonry. Do-it-yourself projects from sun decks to wine cellars are built around 2-by-4s. Indeed, 2-by-4s make up almost 20 per cent of all lumber sold.

But despite appearances, not all 2-by-4s are alike. For one thing, the strength of the 2-by-4 varies greatly according to species and grade of lumber. And none, of course, actually measures 2 inches by 4 inches in cross section. Once many of them did. They were cut to those or somewhat greater dimensions and used rough, as they came from the saw. In this century, however, they began to be planed smooth to something smaller, and eventually the standard 2-by-4 of dry wood measured 1½ inches by 3½ inches when dry and slightly larger when green.

The 2-by-4 as it is now known came into use only after power-operated sawmills of the 19th Century made it economical to rip big logs into uniformly trimmed construction pieces. For many years after American millers began mass-producing dimension lumber including some that was more or less 2 by 4, the regional nature of the sawmill industry led to wide variation. Not until the early 1920s was the first in a series of voluntary softwood lumber standards developed under the auspices of the American Lumber Standards Committee.

Nationwide standardization has been slow, both in the United States and in Canada, where grades and designations are essentially the same. It took nearly 50 years to reach agreement on how to allow for size changes caused by moisture. As lumber dries, it shrinks. Fortunately, its strength increases in greater proportion. Even standards set as recently as 1953 ignored moisture and shrinkage, although about 30 per cent of lumber is sold green. The 2-by-4 was supposed to be 1⅝ by 3⅝, green or dry. One cut to that dimension from green lumber could be counted on to shrink once it was removed from a stack and exposed to air. This source of size discrepancies was finally eliminated in 1970, when the Standards Committee agreed that only lumber containing 19 per cent or less moisture could be sold as dry, and established two official sets of dimensions: 1½ by 3½ for a dry 2-by-4 and 1⁹/₁₆ by 3⁹/₁₆ for a green one.

The width of a 2-by-4 used as a stud is crucial to a smooth-surfaced wall, but the small variations in size do not affect structural strength as much as the kind of wood used, its moisture content and the soundness of the piece. Strength varies surprisingly. A segment of dry southern pine 2-by-4 has borne 7 tons on its end in laboratory tests compared to 3½ tons for an eastern white pine; green 2-by-4s of each species had about a fourth less load-bearing capacity. (These figures only indicate relative strengths; a wall made of 10 dry southern pine 2-by-4s would not necessarily support 70 tons.) Most 2-by-4s are southern pine, Douglas fir or "hem-fir"—a category covering the similar western hemlock and white fir.

The importance of moisture content and species is more than matched by that of grade. Most of the 2-by-4s sold for what is called light framing, which includes most of the ways they are used in house construction, are ranked for their ability to bear stress into four quality grades: construction, stud, standard and utility. The grades are determined by such characteristics as knot size, warp, splits, slope of grain, wane (the beveled edge resulting when a 2-by-4 is milled from the outer portion of a log) and skip (a spot passed over by the plane when the lumber is dressed).

A construction-grade 2-by-4, for example, can have no knot larger than 1½ inches, while a stud-grade 2-by-4 can have a 1¾-inch knot, a standard-grade a 2-inch knot, and the utility-grade a 2½-inch knot. Each piece of graded lumber is usually stamped with its grade, along with a moisture indication of S-GRN or S-DRY, meaning that the surface was green or dry when the 2-by-4 was planed, and the name or an abbreviation of the tree species, such as D. FIR or DOUG. FIR, EASTERN SPRUCE, HEM-FIR, etc.

Often a homeowner can tell simply by looking at a 2-by-4 whether it is suitable for his purpose, whatever its grade may be. For the wall-building described in this book, stud grade generally suffices if the piece needed is no longer than 10 feet. But local building codes may specify the grade of 2-by-4 that must be used for a particular job, depending on the amount of stress the wood will bear. If you are in doubt, insist on structural grade.

The recent more or less uniform standardization of the 2-by-4 has not closed off future modification. The nominal 2-by-4 size itself is being challenged. For walls that do not support the weight of the house, 1-by-4s are sufficient to hold wallboard, and they are accepted by many local codes. Conversely, larger pieces—2-by-6s—have replaced 2-by-4s for some exterior walls because they provide more space for the increased insulation needed to conserve fuel.

In another conservation move—for more efficient use of available timber supplies—composite 2-by-4s have been made up of several short pieces precisely joined together, end to end. One Montana mill showed off the effectiveness of its jointing process by turning out a 2-by-4 that was 400 feet long. A crew of mill hands bent the huge piece into a circle without breaking it. It finally broke when bent sharply around a tree—but not at one of the interlocked and glued joints.

And the good old standard 2-by-4 must change in cross section when the United States and Canada swing over fully to metric measures. The dimensions of the 2-by-4 of the 1970s are almost identical to—but slightly smaller than—the 38 by 89 millimeters that have been recommended as the new metric standard. The 2-by-4 could swell in its next incarnation and emerge as a 38-by-89.

Transforming a Porch into a Year-round Room

Enclosing a porch is easier than building an addition from scratch—and produces a room almost as snug. If the structure is sound, walling in the porch will create new living space you can heat in winter, cool in summer and enjoy all year.

Before you start, check local building regulations and acquire a permit, if you need one. Then strip the porch down to basics: roof, support posts and floor. Take out the ceiling so you can insulate between the joists when you finish the room. If you want the section of house wall that will be inside the new room to match other interior walls, remove any wood or aluminum siding or rough stucco. If the siding is smooth stucco or other masonry, however, you can leave it as is, and put furring strips over it to hold wallboard when you finish the interior.

Enclosing the stripped-down porch be-gins with laying an insulated subfloor. If the existing floor is level wood, you can insulate the underside and cover the top with plywood (page 119). But most porch floors slope to drain off rain so you need to install a framing to compensate for the slope, then insulate between the joists before you put down plywood (right).

Building new exterior walls over the subfloor calls for the same framing techniques used for interior partitions. An exterior door is framed like an interior one; windows are framed similarly, but with sills and cripple studs under the openings. Exterior walls, however, need 2-by-4 fire stops, inserted between the studs, midway from floor to ceiling. The stops retard fires that otherwise would use the stud spaces as chimney stacks.

Finishing the exterior requires adding both sheathing and siding to the walls.

Aluminum siding (pages 116-118) is lightweight enough so you can sheathe the walls inexpensively with asphalt-impregnated board—pressed paper coated with tar that functions as a vapor barrier. With heavier wood siding, you need plywood sheathing covered outside with felt roofing paper. Aluminum siding is available plain or insulated with fiberboard or plastic foam. Both types are installed similarly, but uninsulated siding panels need to be reinforced at the ends with backer plates (page 118).

Once the exterior is complete, most of the steps involved in finishing the interior are familiar ones: wiring, insulating the ceiling and new walls, applying wallboard and covering the subfloor. The only unusual part may be walling over a window opening (page 119) and even that job is only simple carpentry.

Preparing the porch. Using a utility bar, tear down the ceiling and its trim. Remove the frieze boards, if any, but leave the soffit and fascia. Take off any shutters, screens, screen supports, partial walls or railings. Then use a handsaw to cut through the sill of the door from the house, sawing down to the subflooring along the inner edges of the side jambs. Pull the sill out. If you plan to retrim the door, pry off the top and side exterior casings. If you plan to wall over any window, remove it, using the techniques shown on pages 83-84, Steps 1-3.

For wood or aluminum siding, use a circular saw and utility bar to expose the sheathing inside the porch area; be careful not to cut into the sheathing. For a rough-textured stucco-finished house, use a hammer and hacksaw to remove the stucco and the metal lath under it.

Laying a Level Subfloor on a Sloping Slab

1 Attaching the header. To make the new floor flush with the interior floor, measure from the top of the interior subflooring to the slab and deduct ½ inch. Using 2-inch lumber of this width, or ripped to this dimension, cut a header the width of the porch area. (If you do not want the floors to be flush, use at least a 2-by-2 for the header.) Set the header on the slab and attach it to the house wall with 16-penny nails (use cut nails for masonry).

2 Putting up front boards. With metal shears, cut strips of 6-inch aluminum flashing to fit between the header and corner post on each side and between each pair of posts opposite the header. (If the corner posts are inset on the slab, use flashing at least 4 inches wider than the inset.) Lay the strips along the edges of the slab with one side projecting 2 inches, then bend down the projecting flashing. To level the floor, extend a carpenter's line from the top of the header to a corner post and hang a level on the line. Mark the post where the line crosses it. Measure from the outside mark to the slab and use 2-inch lumber ripped to this width for the front boards; cut a front board to fit between each pair of posts. Stand the boards on the flashing, keeping their outer edges flush with outside edges of the posts, and toenail the front boards to the posts. Bend the inner edge of the front flashing up flat against the front board.

INTERIOR FINISHED FLOORING

INTERIOR SUBFLOORING

CONCRETE SLAB

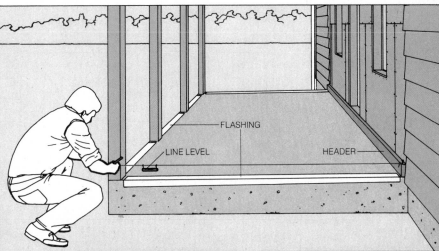

FLASHING

LINE LEVEL

HEADER

FRONT BOARD

HEADER

SIDE JOIST

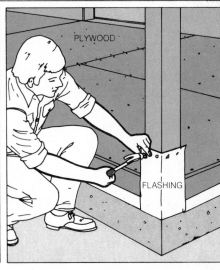

PLYWOOD

FLASHING

3 Laying sleeper joists. For the sleeper joists at the sides of the slab, measure from the header to the corner posts; for intermediate joists, measure to the front boards. Using 2-inch lumber at least as wide as the front boards, cut two side joists and enough intermediate joists to allow for spacing them 16 inches on center. Rip each joist to match the height of the header at one end, the front board or inner post marking at the other end. Toenail the joists to the header and posts, butt-nail them to the front board. Check the top and bottom level of each joist and, if needed, shim underneath so it fits flush against the slab; plane off high spots. Where joists are less than 2½ inches high, secure them to the slab with cut nails. Elsewhere, set 2-by-4 bridges between them and nail the bridges first to the joists, then to the slab. Bend the inner edges of the side flashing up flat against the side joists.

4 Finishing the subflooring. Lay foil-backed insulation batts at least 3 inches thick between the joists. Then cover the subfloor framing with ½-inch plywood, following the procedures on pages 62-63. Finally, to make the bottoms of the posts watertight, fit a strip of aluminum flashing 10 inches long against each post, letting the bottom of the strip extend 2 inches below the framing and the ends overlap the front boards and side joists. Secure the top of the flashing to the posts with galvanized nails.

An Aluminum-clad Exterior

1 **Putting up new walls.** Build wall frames (*pages 28-31*) to fit from the ceiling joists to the subflooring on both sides and the front of the porch. Frame rough openings for the door and windows (*pages 90-91, Steps 1-3*) and add fire stops to the walls by nailing 2-by-4s between each pair of studs about 4 feet from the sole plate. Anchor the frames in place with 16-penny nails.

To sheathe the walls, cut asphalt-impregnated board to fit from the top of each wall frame to about an inch below the bottom of the floor frame. Butt the boards up against the door and window openings. Stagger the joints between boards to avoid four adjoining corners. Attach the sheathing to the wall frames with roofing nails, then install the exterior doors and windows (*pages 86-87 and pages 98-99*).

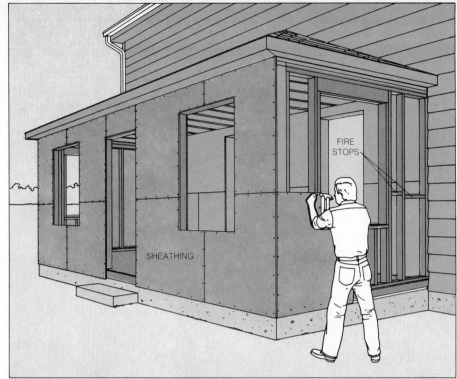

2 **Covering an outside corner.** With metal shears, cut an aluminum outside corner post strip (*inset*) to fit from the top to the bottom of the sheathing. Working at a convenient height, secure the strip to the corner by driving 1½-inch aluminum siding nails into both sides—through the nailing groove or the prepunched holes. Level the strip, then continue inserting nails on both sides at 12-inch intervals.

Caution: Aluminum expands and contracts with heat and cold so the corner posts as well as the other trim and the siding panels should "hang" from the nails. Drive in the nails only to within 1/32 inch of the aluminum. If the nails are too tight, they will make the finished siding ripple like a washboard.

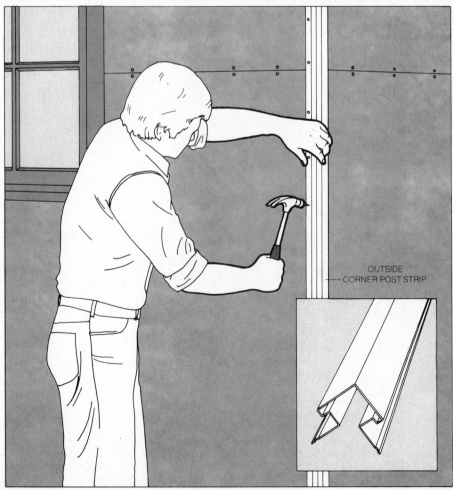

3 **Covering an inside corner.** Cut a strip of aluminum J channel the height of the sheathed wall. Keeping the nailing flange flush with the sheathing, butt the channel as close as possible to the existing aluminum, wood or masonry wall. Straighten the strip with a level, then drive aluminum nails through the flange into the sheathing and stud behind it at 12-inch intervals. Seal the joint between the channel and the wall with rubber-based caulking compound.

4 **Completing the aluminum trim.** Cut continuous strips of J channel to fit around the top and both sides of each exterior door and window. Center each strip above the top casing and bend it down against the sides, notching the nailing flange with metal shears so the channel fits snug around the corners. Secure the channel with aluminum nails. To seal the bottom of a window, cut a strip of general-purpose trim the length of the sill and nail it underneath the sill.

Cut strips of general-purpose trim to fit between the corner post strips at the top of each new wall. With a helper, butt the curved side of the trim against the soffit, level the trim and nail the flange to the sheathing. To piece the trim, leave about ¼ inch between the strips.

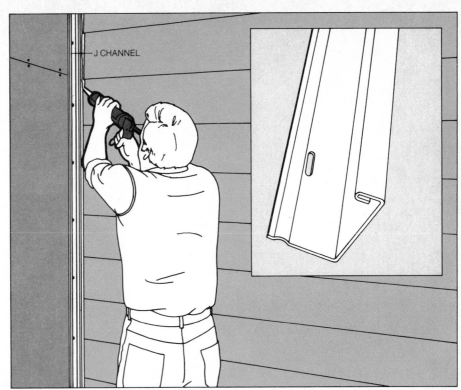

J CHANNEL

J CHANNEL

GENERAL-PURPOSE TRIM

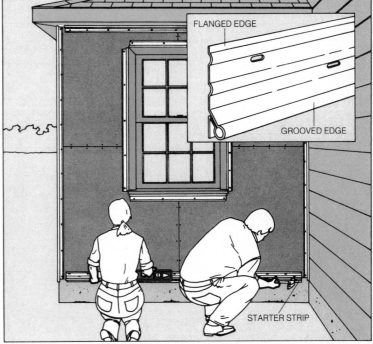

FLANGED EDGE

GROOVED EDGE

STARTER STRIP

5 **Applying the starter strips.** Snap chalk lines about 1½ inches above the bottom of each section of sheathing. Check at the corners to make sure the lines are at the same level around the entire perimeter. Cut a starter strip to the length of each line. Then, with a helper, position the flanged top edge of the starter strip on the chalk line, letting the grooved bottom edge extend below the sheathing. Secure the strip with nails, driven at 8-inch intervals.

6 **Attaching siding panels.** Cut siding panels ½ inch longer than the distance between the projecting edges of the corner strips, or between a corner strip and the J channel around a door or window. To join two panels end to end, allow at least ½ inch for overlap and plan the cutting so you can stagger the joints; notch out ½ inch of the nailing flange on the cut end of one panel so it will slide under the other panel.

Fit the ends of the first panel under the projecting edges of the corner strips or J channel, then lift the panel up until the lower inside lip hooks into the groove in the starter strip. Secure the panel with nails driven into the flange at 16-inch intervals. If the panel is not insulated, insert a backer plate (*inset*) at each end before nailing it. Seat each successive panel similarly, hooking the lip into the groove of the preceding panel.

7 **Shaping the panels.** At windows and above doors, notch the panels before nailing them. Cut through the lip or groove side to the desired depth, then score the panel lengthwise between the cuts. Set a heavy ruler inside the score line and bend the panel over the ruler to break off the unwanted portion. At the soffit, score and break off the top edge of the panel so it will lie under the projecting edge of the attached trim. In most cases the trim will hold the panel edge securely; if not, insert nails near the top of the trim at 18-inch intervals.

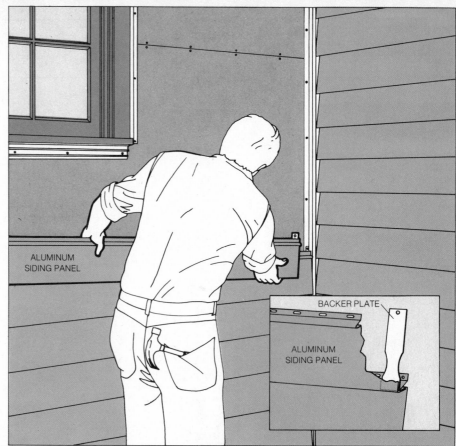

ALUMINUM SIDING PANEL

BACKER PLATE

ALUMINUM SIDING PANEL

Finishing the Interior

A sheathed existing wall. Wire and insulate the new room, then cover the ceiling and walls with wallboard *(pages 36-41 and pages 78-79)*. To close up a window, butt-nail 2-by-4s inside all four sides of the jamb. Then extend the cripple studs above and below it by toenailing a 2-by-4 between the header and rough sill of the opening. Cover the opening with asphalt board before installing wallboard. Inside the house, fill the opening with a wallboard patch *(page 39)*. To retrim the door, extend the top and side jamb flush with the sheathing by attaching ¾-inch-wide wood strips ripped to the required thickness. To replace the door, rip out the jamb and install a prehung unit *(pages 42-45)* or have a professional hang a new door in the old jamb.

A masonry existing wall. Wire and insulate the new room, then cover the ceiling and new walls with wallboard. To put wallboard over all or part of the masonry wall, first install 1-by-3 furring strips spaced 16 inches on center. Attach the strips with cut nails, driven into the mortar joints of bricks or blocks. To hide a window recess, butt-nail 2-by-4 sleepers to the side walls of the opening, keeping the outside edges level with the masonry surface. Toenail two or more 2-by-4s between the sleepers to provide nailing surfaces for the furring strips. Inside the house, extend the cripple studs above and below the window with 2-by-4s before putting wallboard over the opening. At the door, you can nail furring strips inside the recess to install wallboard over the masonry, then retrim the door in the new room with quarter round. To replace the door, rip out the jamb and install a prehung unit or have a professional hang a new door in the old jamb.

Working with a Wood-floored Porch

Prepare the porch *(page 115)*, then saw off the edges of the floor flush with the support frame. If the floor joists are less than 2-by-8, butt-nail a reinforcing joist to each of them—or have a masonry foundation installed after sealing the floor.

Where the floor is level and at the desired height, nail a ½-inch plywood subfloor on top. Then insulate under the porch by pushing 6-inch batts between the joists, vapor-barrier side up, and securing the batts with braces cut from wire hangers to a length a bit longer than the space between joists *(right)*. Cover the ground beneath the porch with strips of 6-mil polyethylene, overlapped by about 6 inches and

weighted down with bricks or stones. (If you cannot crawl under the porch, pry up the floor planks, lay the polyethylene through the joists onto the ground, staple the insulation between the joists, then replace the planks and install the plywood.)

Where the floor slopes, or is lower than the height desired, you do not need to insulate under the porch. Instead install an insulated wood frame on top of the porch floor and cover it with plywood, following the techniques for installing a subfloor over concrete *(page 115, Steps 1-4)*, but using 16-penny nails for the joists. Frame, sheathe and finish the exterior walls *(pages 116-118)*.

A Labor-saving Method for Building a Deck

In pleasant weather a wood deck makes a versatile, sunlit space for a whole family to use. At a fraction of the cost and labor of adding a walled and roofed extension to your house, it provides an outdoor dining room, a play area for children and an entertainment center for adults.

Because a deck represents an extension of an existing structure, it must meet the provisions of your local building code and usually needs a building permit. The low-level deck, about 10 by 12 feet, shown here, is a design that can be assembled and fastened in place by two amateurs. To increase the deck area, additional decks measuring up to 10 by 12 feet can be bolted to this one. The low deck does have one requirement: the ground beneath it must be clear not only of existing structures but also of all plant growth. Then cover the ground with 6-mil polyethylene plastic sheeting.

On the outer edge of cleared ground you must dig holes for posts. The size and depth of these holes are strictly regulated by the building code. Concrete footings for the posts must rest upon undisturbed earth below the frost line, so that freezes and thaws do not warp or crack the wood. Depending on your location and the requirements of your code, the holes you dig may be as shallow as 1 foot or as deep as 6 feet.

At its inner edge the deck is fastened against the house. On a frame house, you must cut the siding away to an outline that exactly matches the rear of the deck frame. The frame can then be bolted through the wall sheathing to a 2-by-6 or 2-by-8 board that runs horizontally behind the sheathing at the level of the house joists. On a solid masonry house, bolt the frame directly to the house *(page 123, Step 4)*.

In choosing the wood, fasteners and finishes for the deck, your main concerns are strength and durability. Ask your lumber supplier to recommend a stiff, non-splintering heartwood with high resistance to decay, wear and warping (some woods that meet these requirements are cypress, Douglas fir, redwood and western red cedar). Buy wood treated with a commercial pressure process in which preservatives are forced deep into the fibers of the wood, or coat the wood yourself with one or another of the standard preservatives commercially available.

Use galvanized lag bolts and nails that are ringed by sharp ridges, spirally grooved or cement coated. An unpigmented or lightly pigmented latex stain or silicone coating will preserve or enhance the color and grain of wood, but for maximum protection of the wood, use urethane porch paint.

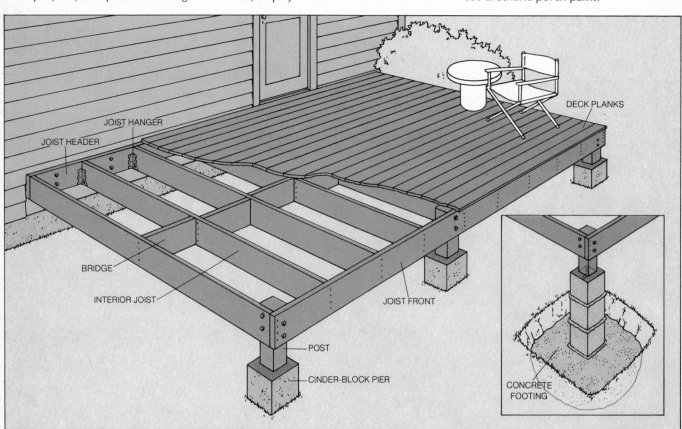

Anatomy of a wood deck. The deck above is bolted to the side of a house. At its outer edge it is supported by posts on solid footings—12-inch slabs of concrete, topped by cinder-block piers. Each pier is filled with concrete and fitted with an anchor bolt; the posts fit onto the anchor bolts, and the deck frame is bolted to the posts. Within the frame, joists are nailed directly to a joist front and are fastened to a joist header by a series of joist hangers. A stag-gered line of bridges gives the frame additional lateral support. The frame supports the finished floor—deck planks spaced ¼ inch apart for drainage and extending 1 inch beyond the edges of the frame for decorative effect.

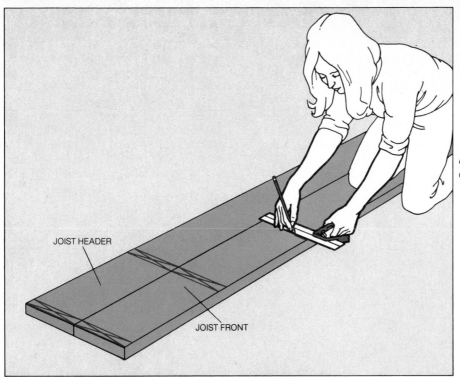

JOIST HEADER

JOIST FRONT

Building the Frame

1 Marking the boards. Using a combination square, mark the joist-header and joist-front boards with the locations of the joists, beginning with a joist at each end of the boards, and spacing the other joists 16 inches from center to center. The last two marks may be less than 16 inches apart, but not more.

2 An open, lightweight frame. Nail the two outermost joists in place between the header and front joists, using four 16-penny cement-coated or grooved-shank nails at each joint. Depending on the wood you use, the four-sided frame will weigh between 120 and 135 pounds—easily liftable by two workers.

Check the structure for squareness with a frame square, then install temporary braces at the outer corners, using 4-foot lengths of 1-by-2 nailed diagonally at each corner. Finally, drill two ¾-inch boltholes through the joist header within each pair of marks for interior joists; the holes should be aligned vertically, 1½ inches from the top and bottom of the header.

JOIST HEADER

BRACE

JOIST FRONT

Installing the Frame

1 **Exposing the sheathing.** On a house with wood or aluminum siding, use a circular saw to cut through the siding just below a doorsill to the outline of the header joist. If necessary, use a crowbar to pry the siding completely free from the sheathing behind it. The sheathing should be clear of nail stubs when you complete this step.

2 **Marking the sheathing.** Using masonry blocks and wood scrap as temporary supports, set the frame into position against the house wall; check its alignment with a level. Using the boltholes you have drilled in the frame as a guide, mark bolthole positions on the sheathing.

3 **Locating the post positions.** Drive two nails 4 inches from each outer corner of the deck frame—one nail on an end joist, the other on the joist front. Extend a string diagonally between each pair of nails, drop a plumb bob from the center of the string and drive a stake at each point where the plumb bob meets the ground.

To locate a third posthole near the center of the joist front—at the angle between it and the center joist—use the mark for the center joist as a guide. Two inches to the left or right of this mark, nail a 3-inch length of 1-by-1 to the joist front, with exactly 2 inches of the 1-by-1 projecting into the frame; be sure that the 1-by-1 makes an exact right angle with the joist front. Drop a plumb bob from the projecting edge of the 1-by-1 and drive a stake at the point where the bob meets the ground.

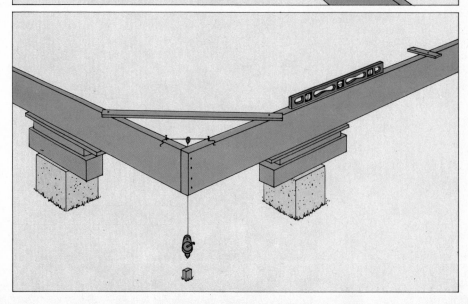

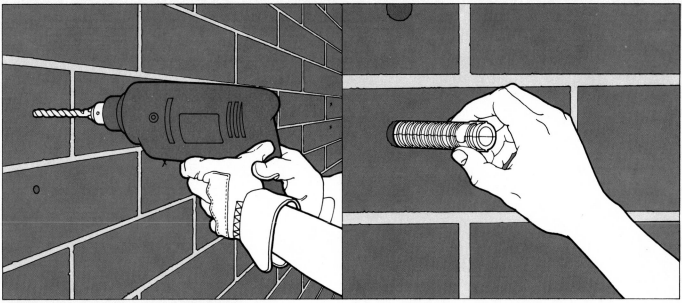

4 **Drilling the boltholes.** With a helper, lift the frame from its template supports and carry it clear of the deck site. In a wood wall, drill ⅜-inch holes at the points you have marked on the sheathing, and fill the holes with caulking. In a masonry wall *(far left, above)*, drill ½-inch holes at these points, using a star drill or an electric drill fitted with a masonry bit. Fill the holes with caulking, then insert a lead expansion anchor in each hole *(above)*.

5 **Pouring the footings.** Using the driven stakes as guides, dig postholes, roughly 16 by 16 inches, to the depth required by your building code—from a minimum of 12 inches to a maximum of several feet. In a wheelbarrow, pre-pare batches of premixed concrete to fill the holes with footings to the depth required by the code. Pour the footings and let the concrete cure for 24 to 48 hours before proceeding.

6 **Bolting the frame to the house wall.** Replace the deck frame on its temporary supports, using a carpenter's level to check its alignment. Then fasten the joist header of the frame to the sheathing or masonry wall of the house with ½-inch lag bolts, each at least 6 inches long; set washers between the boltheads and the joist.

7 **Building a cinder-block pier.** Drop plumb lines over the centers of the postholes (*page 122, Step 3*). In each hole, using the plumb line as a center, trowel an 8-by-8-inch bed of mortar 1½ inches thick on the concrete footing, and lay a hollow-core, corner cinder block on the mortar. Trowel a second 1½-inch mortar bed on the rim of the block, and continue to lay blocks until the block pier rises at least 8 inches above grade. As you work, check the vertical and horizontal alignment of the pier with a level. Fill the posthole with soil to grade level.

8 **Setting post anchors.** Fill the cinder-block cores with concrete and drop a plumb bob to the center of each pier. After an hour or two, when the concrete has begun to set, insert a 6-inch anchor bolt below the plumb bob, leaving 1½ inches of bolt projecting above the concrete. Let the concrete cure for 24 to 48 hours, then cover the top of each pier with termite shield paper—a tar paper coated with copper. The paper not only prevents termite infestation, but keeps the wooden post atop the pier from absorbing moisture from the concrete.

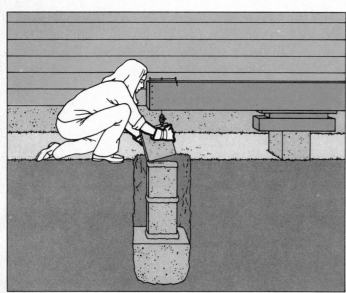

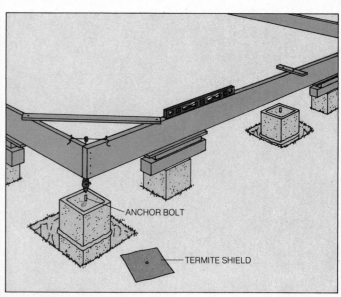

ANCHOR BOLT

TERMITE SHIELD

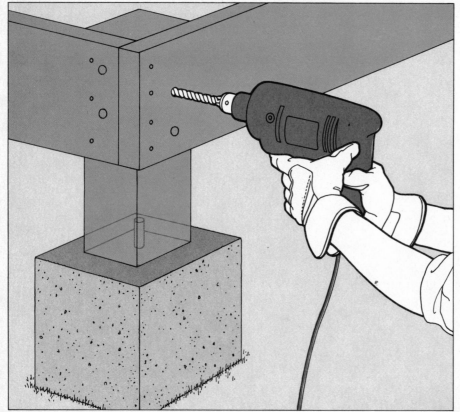

9 **Installing the posts.** Remove the plumb bobs. Cut 4-by-4 posts to fit between the top of each pier and the top of the deck frame. Drill a ½-inch hole 1½ inches into the bottom of each post and slip the post onto an anchor bolt. Nail the post into place with two or three light nails, then drill ⅜-inch boltholes through the frame and into the post. Allow two holes, one above another, for the center post, and four holes, front and side, for each of the corner posts; stagger the holes at the corners so that they do not meet. Secure the posts with ½-inch lag bolts and washers.

BRIDGE

Adding Joists and Deck Boards

1 **A pattern of joists and headers.** Remove the two diagonal frame braces and cover the ground beneath the frame with 6-mil polyethylene, weighted at the edges with bricks or stones and pierced at intervals for drainage. At each of the joist positions marked on the joist header, install a joist hanger *(inset)*, using 1½-inch cement-coated or grooved-shank nails. Install the joists between the header and the joist front, nailing them into the hangers at the header end and driving four 16-penny nails through the front and into each joist at the outer end.

To complete the interior of the frame, install short headers called bridges, each 14½ inches long, between the joists. (If any two joists are less than 16 inches from center to center, cut a shorter header to fit between them.) Set the headers alternately on and just off center, and secure them with four nails at each end.

2 **A pattern of planks.** Cover the deck frame with 2-by-6 planks laid across the joists and fastened at every joist with two 16-penny nails. Allow at least ¼ inch of space between the edges and ends of the planks for drainage; to keep the spacing uniform, use ¼-inch pieces of plywood set on edge as spacers between decking.

Run the decking flush to the house wall, but let it project an inch over the front and sides. Use a professional carpenter's trick to get a straight edge at the sides: lay the decking with an uneven edge an inch or more beyond the side of the frame, snap a chalk line over the planks exactly 1 inch beyond the frame, then saw through all the plank ends along the line.

SPACER

Picture Credits

The sources for the illustrations in this book are shown below. Credits for the pictures from left to right are separated by semicolons, from top to bottom by dashes.

Cover—John Neubauer. 6—John Neubauer. 8,9—Drawings by Vicki Vebell. 10 through 19—Drawings by Ray Skibinski. 20 through 25—Drawings by Dale Gustafson. 26—John Neubauer. 28 through 31—Drawings by Whitman Studio, Inc. 32,33—Drawings by Tom Gladden. 34,35—Drawings by Whitman Studio, Inc. 36 through 41—Drawings by Peter McGinn. 42,43—Drawings by Whitman Studio, Inc. 44,45—Drawings by Vicki Vebell. 46 through 49—Drawings by Forte, Inc. 50 through 57—Drawings by Nick Fasciano. 58—John Neubauer. 60 through 67—Drawings by Peter McGinn. 68 through 77—Drawings by Adolph E. Brotman. 78,79—Drawings by Vicki Vebell. 80—John Neubauer. 82 through 87—Drawings by Forte, Inc. 88 through 91—Drawings by John Sagan. 92 through 97—Drawings by Ray Skibinski. 98 through 101—Drawings by Nick Fasciano. 102,103—Drawings by Vicki Vebell. 104,105—Drawings by Tom Gladden. 106 through 111—Drawings by John Sagan. 112A—John T. Hill/Chimacoff/Peterson Architecture and Urban Design. 112B—Michael Nicholson from Elizabeth Whiting—Tim Sheet Porter from Elizabeth Whiting/Adrian Gale, Architect. 112C—Michael Boys from Susan Griggs Agency. 112D—John Donat/Pierre Botschi, Architect; John T. Hill/Robert A. M. Stern Associates, Architects—John T. Hill/Kevin Durr, Architect. 112E—Norman McGrath/Hanford Yang, Architect. 112F—Carla de Benedetti/Francesco Trabucco and Daniela Volpi, Architects. 112G—Norman McGrath/Benjamin Baldwin, Architect—Jeremy P. Lang/Robert A. M. Stern Associates, Architects. 112H—Norman McGrath/William S. Ehrlich, Architect. 114 through 119—Drawings by Whitman Studio, Inc. 120 through 125—Drawings by Peter McGinn.

The following persons also assisted in the making of this book by preparing the sketches from which the final illustrations were drawn: Fred Collins, Marilyn Dye, Fred Holz, Joan S. McGurren.

Acknowledgments

The index/glossary for this book was prepared by Mel Ingber. The editors also wish to thank the following: Bud Aston, Season-All Industries, Inc., Indiana, Pennsylvania; John Bowden, Washington, D.C.; Eugene Brooks, Interior Superintendent, Richard Poole, General Superintendent, CBI Fairmac Corp., Arlington, Virginia; Gary W. Burke, Sales Order Coordinator, Kwikset Sales and Service Co., Anaheim, California; John Carpenter, Arlington Iron Works, Manassas, Virginia; Kevin Cassidy, James A. Cassidy Co., Beltsville, Maryland; Ron David, Crown Aluminum, Roxboro, North Carolina; R. A. Edgren, Kaiser Aluminum, Home Products Division, Oakland, California; Robert Faulk, Alcoa Building Products, Inc., Landover, Maryland; Bernard E. Friedman, President, Supreme Aluminum Products, Beaver Heights, Maryland; Edward F. Gerber, Milton W. Smithman, National Assoc. of Home Builders, Washington, D.C.; Alec Greenfield, Architect, Head of Architectural Technology Program, Northern Virginia Community College, Annandale, Virginia; Robert Lee Hall, Thomas F. Hall, President, Acme Garage Door, Inc., Washington, D.C.; Gunard E. Hans, Architect, Forest Products Laboratory, Forest Service, United States Dept. of Agriculture, Madison, Wisconsin; Jack Hayes, Yearbook Editor, United States Dept. of Agriculture, Washington, D.C.; Dr. James Hill, Mechanical Engineer, National Bureau of Standards, Washington, D.C.; Robert Holcomb, National Forest Products Assoc., Washington, D.C.; Charles T. Matheson, The Plains, Virginia; Charles Miller, Lothrop Associates Architects, White Plains, New York; Fred M. Schmidt, Season-All Industries, Inc., Indiana, Pennsylvania; Thomas D. Searles, American Lumber Standards Committee, Germantown, Maryland; Barry Stanfield, Hechinger Company, Baileys Cross Roads, Virginia; Peter Stein, Forest History Society, Santa Cruz, California; Hugh Turley, Washington, D.C.; Jack Ullrich, Sales Promotion Manager, Andersen Corp., Bayport, Minnesota.

Index/Glossary

Included in this index are definitions of many of the technical terms used in this book. Page references in italics indicate an illustration of the subject mentioned.

Adhesive: tile, 64; underlayment, 63; wallboard panel, 78; wood-block, 67
Attic: framing walls in, *61;* heating, *104-105;* installing floor in, *61;* insulating, *103;* insulation for, 102

Base shoe: *strip of wood trimming baseboard.* Described, 46; installing, *46-49;* removing, 29
Baseboard: described, 46; installing, *46-49;* removing, 29. *See also* Molding
Beam, collar: *beam run between rafters, used as support for wall or ceiling.* Described, 69; installing, 32, 69
Beam, I: *steel girder used to carry stress in place of load-bearing wall.* Use, 53, 56-57
Bricks: matching color, 110; splitting, 94
BTU: *unit of heat energy.* Described, 104

Carport roof, *18-19*
Ceilings: advantage of new, 59; installing acoustical tile type, 68, *74-77;* installing suspended type, *70-73;* installing wallboard type, 68, *78-79;* preparing attics for, *68-69;* sound absorbing, 58, 59; types, 68
Ceilings, suspended: *ceilings of panels set in a metal grid hung from joists or old ceiling.* Advantages of, 68; installing, *70-71;* installing electrical fixtures in, *72-73;* installing headers under, 10, *12-13*
Channel, F and H: *aluminum channel used to frame storm-door panels.* Described, 20; installing, *22*

Channel, J: *aluminum channel used to protect edge joints of walls.* Installing, *117*

Concrete slab: installing floors on, 60, 61; installing subfloor on porch, *115;* leveling, *60;* moistureproofing, 60, 61

Corner post: *metal sheath protecting outside corner of exterior wall.* Installing, *116*

Cross T: *short metal strip in frame of suspended ceiling.* Installing, *71*

Deck, wood, *120;* building, 81, *120-125;* clearing ground under, *120;* footings, *120;* framing, *121;* installing frame, *122-123;* installing joists, *125;* installing planking, *125;* installing posts and footings, *122, 123-124;* wood for, *120*

Doorframe, building, *34-35*

Doors, accordion: *doors with flexible panels that fold into pleats when door is open.* Described, *10;* installing, *14-15*

Doors, bifold: *doors with hinged rigid panels that fold open.* Described, *6, 7, 10;* installing, *15-16. See also* Header

Doors, exterior, 81; converting from window, *82-87;* installing, *86-87;* prehung units, 82, 88. *See also* Doorways, exterior

Doors, folding and sliding: headers for, *10-13;* installing, 8, *10-17;* as room dividers, 8

Doors, garage: removing, *106-107;* walling-up opening, 106, *108-111*

Doors, interior: installing, *42-43;* installing hardware, *44-45;* prehung units, 34, *42. See also* Doorways, interior

Doors, sliding: described, *10;* installing, *17. See also* Header

Doors, storm. *See* Storm doors

Doorways, exterior: converting from windows in frame house, 81, *82-87;* cutting new, in frame house, 82, *88-90, 92-94;* cutting new, in masonry house, 82, *95-97;* framing, 88, *90-91, 95, 96-97;* locating, 88; for porch enclosure, 116

Doorways, interior: framing, *34-35;* locating, 29

Fascia: *horizontal board between the eaves and the top of a wall; the specialized fascia used for aluminim roofing has a channel along the inner edge to hold the roofing panels.* Described, 18; installing, *18-19*

Fire stops: *horizontal pieces between wall studs, used to retard spread of fire.* Described, 114; installing, *116*

Fixture, troffer: *electrical fixture in the form of an inverted trough serving as a support and reflector for a fluorescent lighting unit.* Described, 72; installing in a suspended ceiling, *72-73*

Fixtures, electrical: adjusting position in ceiling installation, *75, 76;* installing in new walls, 28, *31;* installing recessed type in tile ceiling, *77;* installing in suspended ceiling, *72-73*

Flash patch: *quick drying mortar.* Used to fill subflooring, 62; used to level concrete slab, 60

Flashing: *sheet metal, in strips or specially formed shapes, used to seal joints between differing materials on roof.* Installing on exterior doorway, *86*

Floors: advantages of new, 59; for enclosed porch, 114, *115,* 119; finishing where wall is removed, 50; installing in attic, 60, *61;* installing on concrete, *60, 61,* 81; installing subflooring, *62;* installing tile, *64-66;* installing underlayment, 62, *63;* installing wood-block flooring, *67;* sleepers for, *60, 61*

Furring strips: *thin strips of wood attached to joists or wall serving as anchor points for covering materials.* Installing for insulation of masonry wall, *102;* installing for tile ceiling, *74*

Garage: converting to living space, *106-111;* finishing wall, *110-111;* framing wall, *108-109;* light and ventilation required after conversion, 106; removing door, *106-107;* walling-up doorway, *108-111*

Header: *top support in frame for doorway arch or window opening.* For aluminum storm door, *23, 24;* described, 10; installing when bearing wall is removed, *53-54;* installing across joists, *10-12;* installing in new doorframe, *35;* installing under suspended ceiling, 10, *12-13*

Heaters, space: capacity, 104; electric baseboard, 104; gas, 105; installing electric, *104-105;* thermostat, 105

Insulation, 102; applying, *102-103;* batts, 102; blankets, 102; for enclosed porch, 114; rigid panels, *102*

Joint knife: *broad bladed tool used to apply joint compound.* Described, 36; use, *40*

Joint compound: *plaster-based filler and adhesive used at wallboard joints.* Applying, 36, *40;* handling, 37; used on wallboard ceiling, 79

Joists: *horizontal structural beams supporting ceilings and floors.* Attaching headers to, *11-13;* location, 10; reinforcing, 60, *61;* sleepers, *60, 61*

Joist, false: *nonstructural beam used in installation of ceiling.* Installing, *74*

Lintel: *load-bearing horizontal beam above masonry doorway, arch or window opening.* Set in block wall, *96;* set in solid brick wall, *95;* set in brick veneer wall, *93-94*

Lockset: *hardware for door latch and lock.* Described, 42; installing, *44-45*

Lofts, 112, *112A, 112D*

Lumber, dimension: grades, 113; standards, 113; strength, 113; 2-by-4, 113

Mastic: *viscous adhesive.* Use on wood-block flooring, 67

Molding: *strips of wood trim.* Described, *46;* installing, *46-49;* installing on tile ceiling, *76;* joints, *47;* old, *49. See also* Baseboard

Nails, coated box: *nails coated with adhesive resin.* Used for fastening underlayment, 63

Nails, underlayment: *nails with broad thin heads.* Used for fastening underlayment, 63

Outdoor spaces, enclosing, 81; porch, *114-119;* with ready-made units, *20-25*

Panels, acoustical: *sound-absorbing panels.* Described, 68; fragility, 68

Pans, roof: *metal panels used for roofing.* Described, 18

Partitions. *See* Walls

Patio: *building aluminum panel enclosure, 20-25;* installing door in enclosure, *23-25;* roof, *18-19. See also* Deck; Porch

Plate, sole: *bottom beam to which partition frame is anchored.* Described, 28; installing, *28, 30-31;* installing in attic, *32;* removing, *52*

Plate, top: *top beam of wall frame.* Described, 28; installing, *28-29;* removing from bearing wall, *54*

Porch: converting into a room, *114-119;* enclosing wood-floored type, 119; erecting enclosure walls, *116-117;* finishing pre-existing wall of enclosure, *119;* insulating floor, 114; insulating roof, 114; laying wood subfloor on slab, *115;* siding enclosure, *118;* stripping to basics, 114. See also Deck; Patio

Roofs, for patios and carports, *18-19;* aluminum panels for, 18; installing, *18-19*

Room dividers, ready-made, 7, 8; folding and sliding doors, 8, *10-17;* shelving, *8-9*

Runners: *long metal strips in frame of suspended ceiling.* Described, 70; installing, *71*

Sheathing: *layer under siding on exterior wall.* Applying, 110; types and siding, 110, 114

Shelving: as room dividers, 8; anchoring pole-type, 8, *9;* anchoring storage units, *8*

Siding: for porch enclosure, 114, *118;* for walled-up garage doorway, 106, *110-111;* shaping, 118. See also Sheathing

Sleepers: *floor joists laid on concrete slab.* Described, 60; installing, *61;* installing on porch slab, *115*

Sound, transmission and wall sheathing, 28. See also Tile, sound absorbing

Space: building-in units, 112D; and color, *112B, 112C;* creative use of, 112, *112A-112H;* dividing, *112D-112E;* and glass, *112B;* and light, *112F, 112H;* lofts, *112A, 112D;* and mirrors, 112B; open plan, 112; opening walls, *112F-112G;* perspective, *112B*

Storm doors: installing in aluminum panel walls, 23-25; as panels for enclosing patio, *20-25;* transom for, *24-25*

Studs: *vertical supports within walls.* Cripple, *35;* framing doorway with, *34-35;* framing wall with, *29-31;* jack, *35;* rewiring when dismantling wall, *51*

Subflooring: *rough flooring laid over joists to serve as base for finished floor.*

Described, 60; filling surface, 62; installing, *62;* plywood, 62

Termite shield, *109*

Threshold, transitional: *metal plate used as joint between two types of flooring.* Use, 67

Tiles, acoustical: *sound-absorbing tiles.* Fragility, 68; installing as ceiling, *58, 59, 74-77;* installing recessed electrical fixture in, *77;* installing in suspended ceiling, *70, 71;* trimming for electrical fixture, *76.* See also Ceilings

Tiles, flooring: base for, 60; cutting, *66;* dry run, *64-65;* installing, *64-66;* installing underlayment for, *62, 64;* self-sticking, 64; types, 64

Toenailing: *fastening two pieces of lumber with nails at an angle.* Described, 28; studs and plates, 31

Transom: installing over aluminum panels, *24-25*

Underlayment: *smooth-surfaced base for floor tiles or linoleum.* Hardboard, 62; installing, *62, 63;* plywood, 62; methods of fixing, 63

Wall, knee: *wall meeting low end of sloped ceiling.* Building, *32;* height, 68; insulating, *103*

Wall panels, aluminum, for enclosing patio, *20-22*

Wallboard: *panels of gypsum plaster, sandwiched between sheets of paper, used for walls and ceilings.* Cutting, *36-37;* described, 68; handling tips, 37; installing on ceiling, *78-79;* installing horizontally, 37, *39;* installing on sloped ceiling, 36; installing on walls, *36-41;* joints, *40-41;* nailing, 26, 27, *38;* replacing, 39; replacing plaster with, *39;* sound insulating qualities, 28; trimming for fixtures or ducts, 79

Walls: converting exterior to interior when enclosing porch, 114, *119;* effects of placement, 27; installing moldings, *46-49;* joints of enclosed porch, *46, 117;* removal of baseboard and molding, 29;

removing, 50; replacing plaster with wallboard, 39; temporary support, *53;* wiring, pipes and ducts within, 50

Walls, exterior: fire stops, 114, for porch enclosure, 117, *116-119;* insulating attics, *103;* insulating masonry, *102;* opening aluminum sides, 88; opening bearing, 88; opening brick veneer, 88, *92-94;* opening masonry, 88, *95-97;* opening stucco, *88-90;* patio enclosure of ready-made units, *20-25;* replacing garage door, *106-111;* siding new wall, *110-111*

Walls, interior bearing: *walls helping support weight of house.* Beams replacing, 53, *54-55, 56-57;* described, 27, 50; girder replacing, 53, *56-57;* removing, 50, *53-57;* removing section of, *56;* transmission of load when wall is removed, 53, *54*

Walls, interior nonbearing: *walls not supporting house.* Building frame, *28-31;* building frame in attic, *32-33;* described, 27, 50; installing between joists, 28, *29;* planning, 27; removing, 50, *51-52;* removing section, *52, 112F, 112G*

Windows: box frame for metal replacement type, *100-101;* converting to doorways, 81, *82-87;* cutting frame house for, *88-90, 92-94;* cutting masonry house for, *95-97;* double hung, 98, *100;* framing in brick masonry, *95, 97;* framing in frame house, *90-91;* framing in masonry block, *96-97;* installing prehung, *90-91, 98-99, 100-101;* metal replacement, 98, *100-101;* for porch enclosures, 116; prehung, 81; removing, *82-84;* walling-up, 114, *119*

Wiring: electric baseboard heaters, *104-105;* installing in new walls, 28, *31;* removing when dismantling walls, 51; three-wire receptacle, *105;* thermostat, *105*

Wood-block flooring, 67; installing, 67

Z bar: *hardware serving as weather seal on storm door.* Installing, *23, 24*